TRUE or FALSE?

Written by
Andrea Mills

Consultants:
**Richard Walker (Human body), Kim Bryan (Nature and Earth),
Jack Challoner (Science and technology), Carole Stott (Space),
and Susan Kennedy (History and culture)**

DK

LONDON, NEW YORK, MUNICH,
MELBOURNE, and DELHI

Senior editor Andrea Mills
Senior designer Sheila Collins
Editorial assistant Ciara Heneghan

Additional editorial assistance Carron Brown,
Steven Carton, Matilda Gollon, Victoria Pyke
Additional design assistance Paul Drislane,
Jim Green, Stefan Podhorodecki, Mary Sandberg

Managing art editor Michael Duffy
Managing editor Lin Esposito

Illustrators Adam Benton, Stuart Carter Jackson
Creative retouching Steve Willis

Jacket design Mark Cavanagh
Jacket editor Maud Whatley
Jacket design development manager
Sophia M Tampakopoulos Turner
Senior producer Ben Marcus
Production controller Gemma Sharpe

Publisher Andrew Macintyre
Art director Phil Ormerod
Associate publishing director Liz Wheeler
Publishing director Jonathan Metcalf

DK India
Project art editor Deep Shikha Walia
Art editors Shipra Jain, Isha Nagar
Project editor Bharti Bedi
Managing editor Alka Thakur
Managing art editor Romi Chakraborty

Senior picture researcher Sumedha Chopra
Senior DTP designer Neeraj Bhatia
DTP designer Nityanand Kumar
Production manager Pankaj Sharma

First published in Great Britain in 2014
by Dorling Kindersley Limited
80 Strand, London WC2R 0RL

Copyright © 2014 Dorling Kindersley Limited

A Penguin Random House Company

1 3 5 7 9 10 8 6 4 2
001–187013–10/14

A CIP catalogue record for this book
is available from the British Library.

ISBN: 978-1-4093-4795-8

Printed and bound in China by Hung Hing

Discover more at
www.dk.com

CONTENTS

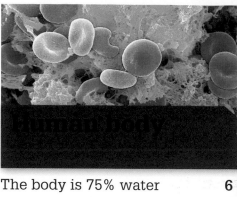

Human body

Nature

Science and technology

Space

Earth

History and culture

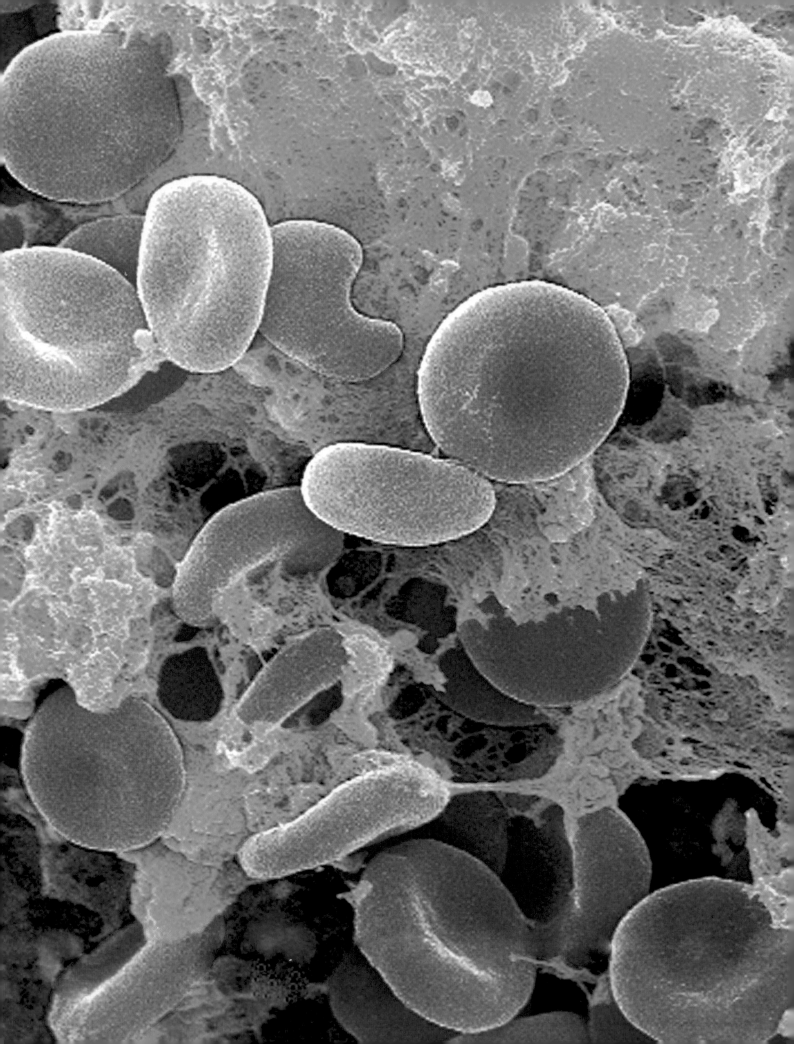

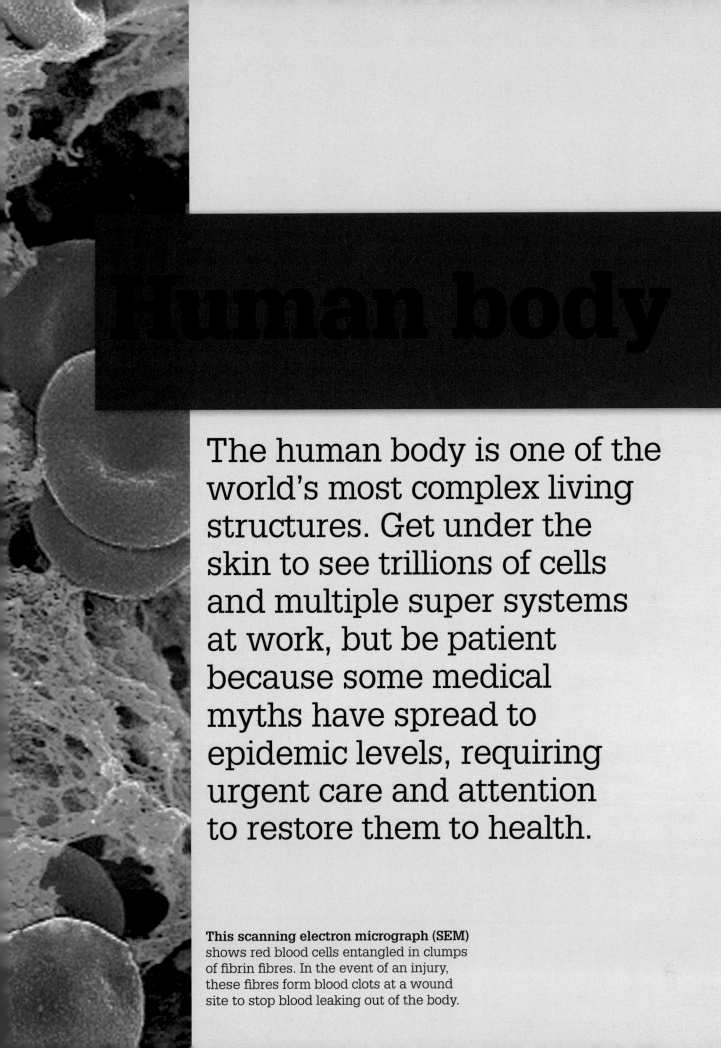

Human body

The human body is one of the world's most complex living structures. Get under the skin to see trillions of cells and multiple super systems at work, but be patient because some medical myths have spread to epidemic levels, requiring urgent care and attention to restore them to health.

This scanning electron micrograph (SEM) shows red blood cells entangled in clumps of fibrin fibres. In the event of an injury, these fibres form blood clots at a wound site to stop blood leaking out of the body.

TRUE or FALSE?

The body is 75% water

Water is not just the world's best thirst-quencher. It is essential to your life on Earth. More than **75 per cent** of a baby's body weight is water. Adult males are **60 per cent** water, while females are **50 per cent**. About **65 per cent** of the body's water is in its **40 trillion cells**.

Is it possible to die from drinking too much water?

When the body's water levels fall, the brain's hypothalamus recognizes the drop and triggers the thirst response. Losing 10 per cent will leave you seriously ill.

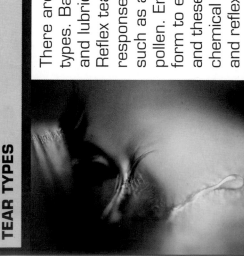

TEAR TYPES

There are three tear types. Basal tears clean and lubricate the eyes. Reflex tears are in response to an irritant, such as an onion or pollen. Emotional tears form to express feelings, and these have a different chemical make-up to basal and reflex tears.

Newborn babies have the highest water content at 75 per cent. That's because they have proportionally much more water in their tissue fluid and blood than adults do.

The amount of sweat produced by the body depends on the number of sweat glands – ranging between two and four million per person.

Elderly people have the lowest water content at 45 to 50 per cent. As people age, fat tissue replaces lean muscle. Unlike muscle and most other tissues, fat tissue contains just 10 to 15 per cent water, hence an older person's lower water content.

The body gains and loses water constantly. Water is taken into the body in food and drink. Water is lost from the body in four main ways. Every day an average adult loses about 1.5 litres (2.6 pt) of water in urine, 0.5 litres (0.9 pt) in sweat, 0.4 litres (0.7 pt) breathing out, and 0.1 litres (0.2 pt) in faeces (poo). Water loss is constantly adjusted to match water gain in order to maintain a steady water balance inside the body.

Blood is 83 per cent water, muscle is 75 per cent water, fat is 10 to 15 per cent water, and bone is 22 per cent water.

FAST FACTS

THE HUMAN BODY CONTAINS
ABOUT
5 LITRES
(8.8 PINTS) OF

BLOOD

This accounts for about 7 per cent of the body's weight. People belong to one of four main blood groups, or types. These are A, B, AB, and O. Each of these can be either RhD positive or RhD negative, so your blood group can be one of eight different types.

OUR SALIVARY GLANDS PRODUCE
ABOUT
1.5 LITRES
(2.6 PINTS)
OF SALIVA
EVERY DAY

As saliva is released gradually, we swallow it bit by bit without realizing. Human saliva is 99 per cent water and 1 per cent other substances.

TRUE or FALSE? We use only 10% of our brains

This is a mad myth from the **19th century**, when scientists had many strange ideas about the human brain. In fact, sensors and scanners reveal that we use **all of our brain,** and most tasks involve **activity in many different areas** at the same time.

Premotor cortex initiates, guides, and coordinates actions.

Prefrontal cortex is the main area associated with personality, thinking, and awareness.

Broca's area controls speech and the formation of words.

The auditory association cortex links sound signals with memories, emotions, and other senses.

Scientists have mapped areas of the brain responsible for tasks such as seeing, hearing, speaking, and movement. But consciousness, memory, and learning do not seem to be related to particular areas – they may involve activity in many parts of the brain at once.

BRAIN AT WORK

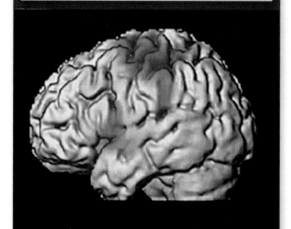

MRI scans can show when parts of the brain are active. The areas in red above indicate activity in the left brain when a right finger is moved. These include parts of the premotor cortex and primary motor cortex, and the cerebellum, which coordinates movements.

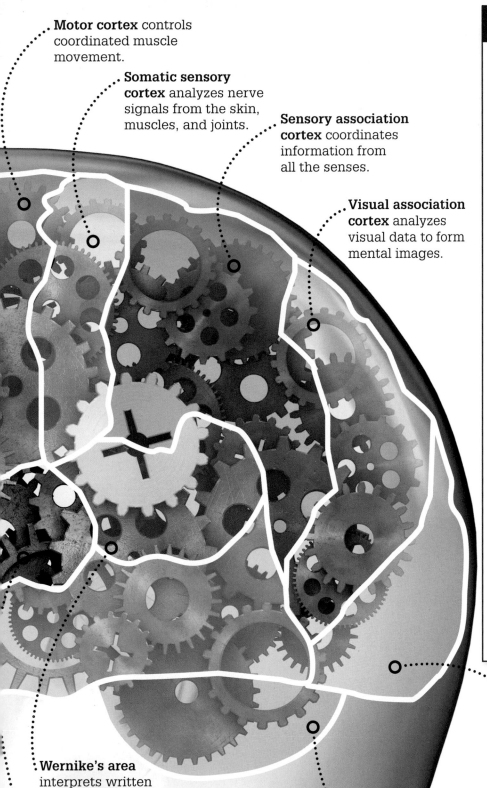

Motor cortex controls coordinated muscle movement.

Somatic sensory cortex analyzes nerve signals from the skin, muscles, and joints.

Sensory association cortex coordinates information from all the senses.

Visual association cortex analyzes visual data to form mental images.

Wernike's area interprets written and spoken language.

Primary auditory cortex analyzes nerve signals from the ears.

Cerebellum helps control balance and movement.

Primary visual cortex receives visual information from the eyes.

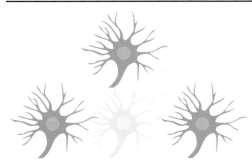

FAST FACTS

THE BRAIN DOESN'T FEEL PAIN

Headaches are caused by other pain-sensitive structures that surround the brain. Brain tissue itself lacks pain receptors, which is why brain surgery can be carried out while patients are awake.

IF A BRAIN CELL DIES, IT MAY BE REPLACED

It was once believed that the brain grew and developed only during childhood and adolescence. Now it is known that human brains are constantly changing in various ways, including replacing some damaged cells.

Are people with larger brains more intelligent?

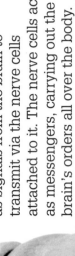

Divided by a groove, the brain has two halves – the left and right hemisphere, each responsible for the opposite half of the body.

The left hemisphere controls the right side of the body and oversees language and maths skills.

The right hemisphere controls the left side of the body and manages creativity and spatial awareness.

The brain is the control centre for the nervous system, responsible for all nerve activity inside the body. The spinal cord receives instructions as signals from the brain to transmit via the nerve cells attached to it. The nerve cells act as messengers, carrying out the brain's orders all over the body.

TRUE or FALSE?

The brain's left side controls the body's right side

You're a bundle of nerves! That's because the brain and spinal cord use billions of **whizzy nerve cells** to send instructions around the body. The **brain's left side** controls the **body's right side**, and vice versa.

Damage to one side of the brain will affect the opposite side of the body.

The sciatic nerve supplies the hamstring muscles at the back of the thigh. It is the body's thickest and longest nerve.

NEURON NETWORK

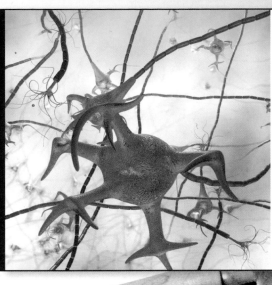

The brain contains about 100 billion microscopic nerve cells called neurons, which each have connections with thousands of other neurons. These neurons have "tails" that receive or transmit electrical nerve impulses from or to other neurons. They create and send more messages than all the telephones in the world.

When the tendon below the kneecap is tapped, a sudden kicking movement of the lower leg results. This knee-jerk reflex is used by doctors to check that the nervous system is working normally.

Branches of the sciatic nerve control muscles in the lower leg and foot.

The ulnar nerve supplies some of the muscles that move the wrist and the fingers.

What percentage of the global population is right-handed?

▣ FAST FACTS

LAID END TO END, ALL THE NEURONS IN THE HUMAN BODY WOULD REACH THE MOON

MOON

Neurons laid end to end

EARTH

Neurons (nerve cells) are microscopic, with each one measuring about 10 microns (1/100th of a mm) wide. However, you have so many, and some are so long, that if they were laid end to end, they would extend to about 380,000 km (236,000 miles).

REFLEX ACTIONS BYPASS THE BRAIN

SIGNAL reaches brain and pain is felt only after hand pulls away

IMPULSES from spinal cord make arm muscle contract

WITHDRAWAL REFLEX moves hand away

In many reflex actions nerve signals travel through the spinal cord but not the brain. If you touch something hot, your hand moves away automatically without brain involvement.

TRUE or FALSE? We lose most body heat through our heads

Only **9 per cent** of the body's surface area is head, and the heat lost from here is **10 per cent**. However, the head and chest are **five times more sensitive** to temperature change than the rest of the body. This makes it feel that covering them up does more to stop heat loss.

FREEZING FROSTBITE

Like other body areas, the fingers and toes are kept warm by blood flowing through them. But exposed to freezing conditions, they lose heat rapidly and blood vessels narrow. This stops blood flow, so their tissues die. The resulting damage is called frostbite.

If we get too cold, blood vessels in the skin's dermis narrow to minimize heat loss, and we get goosebumps.

If we start to overheat, blood vessels in the skin's dermis widen to lose heat, and sweat evaporates from the skin's surface to cool the body down.

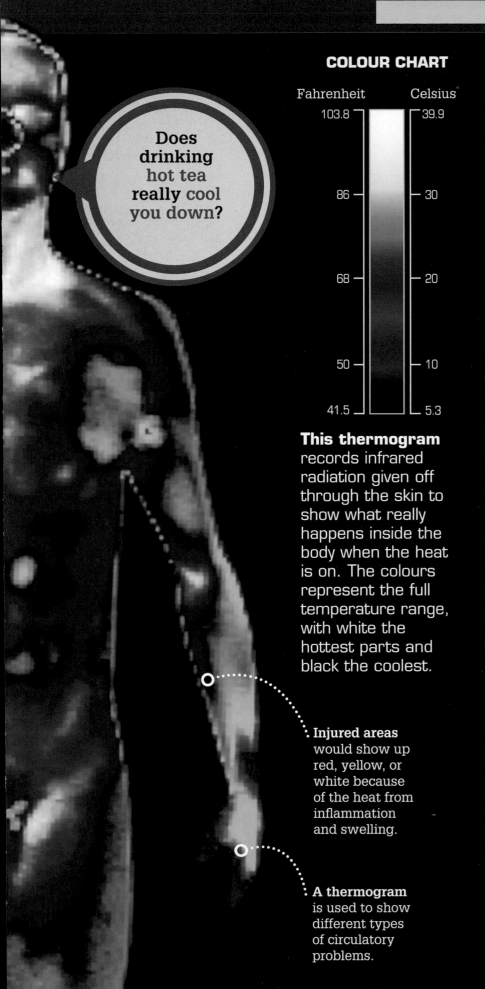

Does drinking hot tea really cool you down?

COLOUR CHART

Fahrenheit		Celsius
103.8		39.9
86		30
68		20
50		10
41.5		5.3

This thermogram records infrared radiation given off through the skin to show what really happens inside the body when the heat is on. The colours represent the full temperature range, with white the hottest parts and black the coolest.

Injured areas would show up red, yellow, or white because of the heat from inflammation and swelling.

A thermogram is used to show different types of circulatory problems.

FAST FACTS

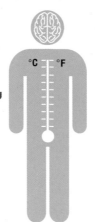

THE BRAIN REGULATES BODY TEMPERATURE, WORKING TO MAINTAIN A CONSTANT 37°C (98.6°F)

A part of the brain called the hypothalamus acts as a thermostat for the body. If the body becomes too hot or cold, the hypothalamus will stimulate a response to return it to normal temperature.

PLACED IN A STRAIGHT LINE, YOUR CIRCULATORY SYSTEM COULD ORBIT EARTH TWO AND A HALF TIMES

If all your arteries, veins, and capillaries were laid out end to end, the total length would be about 100,000 km (60,000 miles). Capillaries make up about 98 per cent of this length.

THE HEART BEATS ABOUT THREE BILLION TIMES IN AN AVERAGE LIFETIME

Regular exercise helps to keep your heart fit and healthy. During exercise, your heart rate increases to pump extra blood, and the oxygen and fuel it carries, to the muscles that move you.

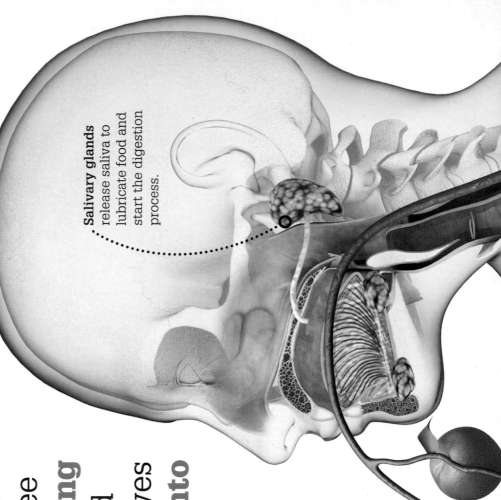

Salivary glands release saliva to lubricate food and start the digestion process.

If you swallow an apple pip, a tree will grow in your stomach

Your tummy does not provide a **suitable environment** for a tree to grow. Instead, pips **pass along** your intestines, and are pushed outside in faeces. If a pip survives this journey, it may yet **grow into a tree**, using sunlight energy.

APPENDIX DEFENCE

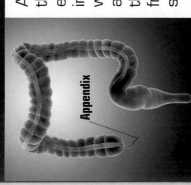

Appendix

Attached to the large intestine, the appendix is used by plant-eating animals to digest cellulose in plants. But for a long time it was a mystery why people had appendixes. It is now known that this organ helps defend the body from attack by germs, and also stores "friendly" gut bacteria.

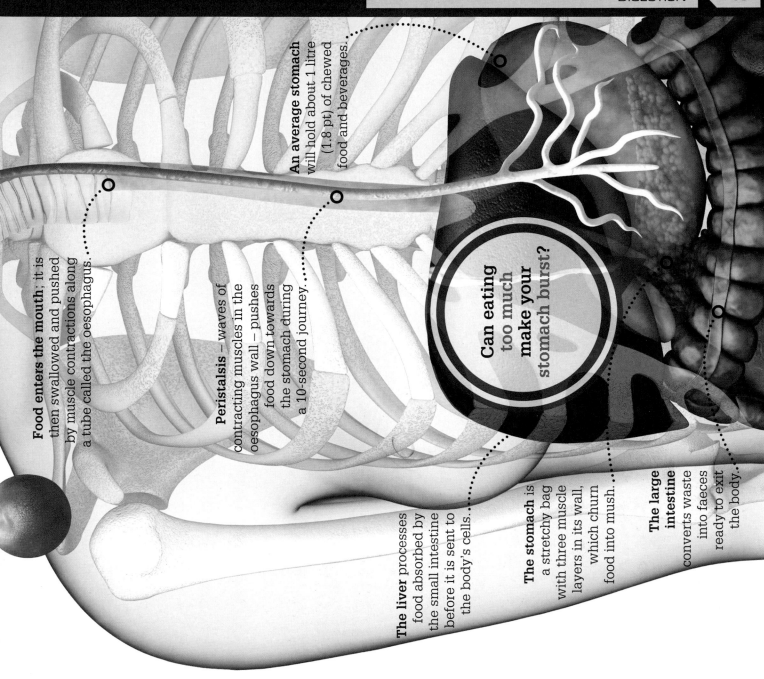

Food enters the mouth; it is then swallowed and pushed by muscle contractions along a tube called the oesophagus.

An average stomach will hold about 1 litre (1.8 pt) of chewed food and beverages.

Peristalsis – waves of contracting muscles in the oesophagus wall – pushes food down towards the stomach during a 10-second journey.

Can eating too much make your stomach burst?

The liver processes food absorbed by the small intestine before it is sent to the body's cells.

The stomach is a stretchy bag with three muscle layers in its wall, which churn food into mush.

The large intestine converts waste into faeces ready to exit the body.

Nutrients are needed for the body to develop and thrive. Food travels through the digestive system where it is broken down to release the necessary nutrients. Passing through the small intestine, nutrients are absorbed into the blood and carried, by way of the liver, to body cells that need them. What is left of the food becomes waste in the intestines before it leaves the body, completing the digestive process.

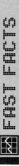

FAST FACTS

THE AVERAGE PERSON EATS THE WEIGHT OF A SPERM WHALE IN FOOD IN A LIFETIME

That's a whopping 40 tonnes! In Western society, we consume about 1.4 kg (3 lb) of food daily. We also drink about 44,000 litres (9,680 gallons) over the course of our lives, which works out at 1.5 litres (2.6 pints) a day.

STOMACH ACID IS STRONG ENOUGH TO STRIP PAINT

Cells in the stomach lining release hydrochloric acid, which is needed to digest proteins. The stomach lining itself is not affected by this strong acid because other cells produce mucus that coats the lining, forming a physical barrier that prevents the acid digesting it.

The skull consists of 22 bones, with 21 of them locked together. Only the lower jaw (mandible) can move.

There are 12 pairs of ribs, 10 of which are attached to the sternum (breastbone) by flexible cartilage.

The backbone is a column of 26 bones called vertebrae that are linked by shock-absorbing cartilage discs.

You are taller in the morning than the evening

This is not a **tall story** – we are bigger in bed. The backbone doesn't have to support body weight, so discs between vertebrae are not squashed as in the day. **The long and the short of it** is we are 0.5 cm (0.2 in) taller in the morning and 0.5 cm (0.2 in) smaller by evening.

SPONGY CENTRE

Bones are a mix of calcium salts and flexible collagen. The outer tissue, called compact bone, is dense and hard. The interior, called spongy bone (pictured), is lightweight yet resilient. Resembling honeycomb, it can withstand everyday stresses and strains.

Each hand has 27 bones and multiple movable joints called knuckles.

The pelvic (hip) girdle attaches the legs to the skeleton via the hip joints.

The femur (thighbone) is the longest bone in the human body, running from the pelvic girdle to the knee joint.

About 400 joints connect the bones, which are held together by strong tissue called ligaments.

The skeleton is an intricate wonderland of 206 bones, supporting and shaping the human body. As strong as steel but one-sixth as heavy, bone makes the skeleton both solid and flexible. It protects the soft organs of the body, including the brain and lungs, and provides movement when muscles pull on the bones.

Bones make up 20 per cent of the body's mass.

Where in the human body are one quarter of all the bones located?

The tibia (shinbone) extends from the knee to the ankle and supports the body's weight.

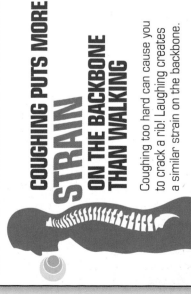

BONES ARE CONSTANTLY RESHAPING THEMSELVES

The entire human skeleton is replaced every 10 years. This gradual process involves teams of cells removing old bone tissue and making new bone tissue. In the process, bones are constantly reshaped to give them optimal strength.

ASTRONAUTS GROW TALLER IN SPACE

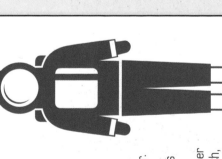

When the backbone is not exposed to the pull of Earth's gravity, it gets longer. This is because the discs that separate the backbone's vertebrae are no longer compressed (squashed). After an astronaut returns to Earth, it takes months for the backbone to go back to its normal length.

COUGHING PUTS MORE STRAIN ON THE BACKBONE THAN WALKING

Coughing too hard can cause you to crack a rib! Laughing creates a similar strain on the backbone.

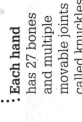

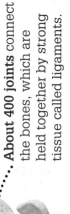

TRUE or FALSE? You use more muscles to frown than to smile

Keep smiling! Though smiling actually uses more muscles than frowning, it takes **less effort**. Most of us **smile much more often** than we frown, so our smile muscles stay in **better shape**.

Frontalis muscle raises the eyebrows, causing the forehead to wrinkle.

Levator labii superioris muscle lifts and curls the upper lip.

Zygomaticus major and minor muscles pull the corner of the mouth upwards, backwards, and outwards.

Risorius muscle pulls the corner of the mouth to the side and backwards to create a smile.

MAKING MUSCLE

Scientists have found a way to regenerate human skeletal muscle using pig proteins. This can help people injured in accidents or wars avoid amputation. Proteins taken from pig intestines are placed inside the damaged tissue. Human stem cells move to the protein and begin to grow matching bone and tissue.

Is it true that smiling is contagious?

Orbicularis oculi muscle closes the eyelids, as well as producing blinks and winks.

The way you are feeling is written all over your face, thanks to 42 muscles. These pull on your skin in different ways to create a range of expressions, from a winning smile to an angry scowl. People all over the world recognize the same six facial expressions – happiness, sadness, fear, surprise, anger, and disgust.

Corrugator supercilii muscle wrinkles the forehead into a frown.

Procerus muscle draws eyebrows together and downwards.

Depressor muscles pull the corner of the mouth downwards.

Mentalis muscle wrinkles the chin, resulting in the lower lip pushing out.

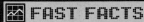
FAST FACTS

THE **BIGGEST** AND STRONGEST MUSCLE IN YOUR BODY SHAPES **YOUR BOTTOM**

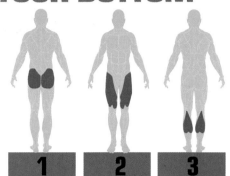

1	**2**	**3**
GLUTEUS MAXIMUS (BUTTOCKS)	QUADRICEPS FEMORIS (THIGH)	SOLEUS (CALF)

The gluteus maximus fights against gravity to pull your body upwards when you get up from a seat, run, or walk up stairs. Other strong muscles are found in the thigh, the calf, the jaw, and the tongue.

THE SMALLEST **MUSCLE** IS IN THE **EAR**

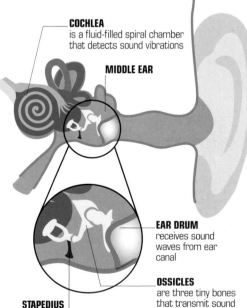

COCHLEA is a fluid-filled spiral chamber that detects sound vibrations

MIDDLE EAR

EAR DRUM receives sound waves from ear canal

OSSICLES are three tiny bones that transmit sound waves to inner ear

STAPEDIUS MUSCLE

The stapedius, inside the middle ear, measures about 1 mm (0.04 in) long and plays a part in sound transmission. It helps to prevent loud sounds damaging the ear's delicate receptors.

TRUE or FALSE? Your irises are as unique as your fingerprints

Here's an **eye-opener** – everyone has a unique iris pattern. This **coloured ring** around the pupil is as individual as your fingerprints, ensuring we're all complete **one-offs**.

The iris is so complex and multi-layered that even your right and left eyes are different. Identical twins also have different iris patterns.

IRIS RECOGNITION

As every person has a unique iris pattern, iris recognition software has been developed for identification purposes. A scan of the pupil converts the iris pattern into a digital code, which is stored in a database with other people's unique codes.

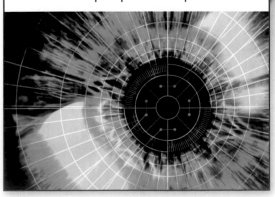

What do all blue-eyed people have in common?

The tough, outer layer is the sclera, responsible for keeping the shape of the eye.

Sight is the most important sense, enabling us to view the world. Light from exterior objects is automatically focused onto a layer of light receptors at the back of the eye. These receptors then send messages to the brain about the patterns of light. The brain interprets these messages, enabling us to "see" 3D, moving colour images of what is going on around us.

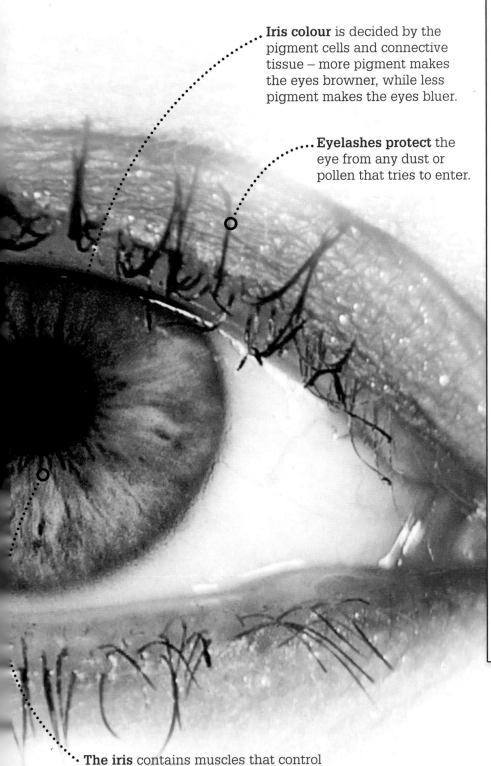

Iris colour is decided by the pigment cells and connective tissue – more pigment makes the eyes browner, while less pigment makes the eyes bluer.

Eyelashes protect the eye from any dust or pollen that tries to enter.

The iris contains muscles that control the levels of light entering the pupil.

FAST FACTS

THE EYE CAN DISTINGUISH BETWEEN UP TO 10 MILLION DIFFERENT COLOURS

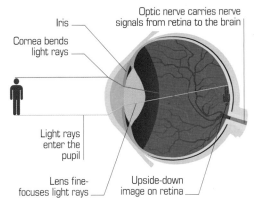

Iris

Optic nerve carries nerve signals from retina to the brain

Cornea bends light rays

Light rays enter the pupil

Lens fine-focuses light rays

Upside-down image on retina

The pupil is not a black circle but a hole in the iris that lets light enter the eye. Light rays are focused by the cornea and lens to produce an image on the retina. We see in colour because light-sensitive cells in the retina respond to different colours and send signals to the brain.

THERE ARE MORE COLOUR-BLIND BOYS THAN GIRLS

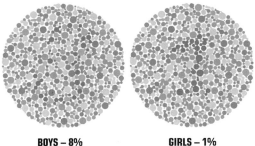

BOYS – 8%　　　**GIRLS – 1%**

People with red/green colour blindness – the most common form – find it hard to distinguish colours that have a red or green element to them. Colour-blind people often have an increased ability to spot camouflaged objects, and excellent night vision.

TRUE or FALSE? The tongue has taste zones

Taste maps took off in the 20th century, when it was thought the tongue could be divided into **taste zones**. But then scientists discovered that different tastes can be **detected everywhere** on the tongue – so there really is no accounting for taste!

TASTE BASE

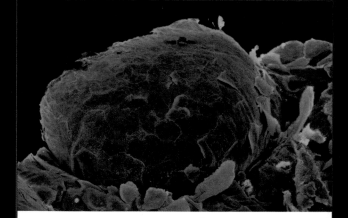

The tongue is covered in microscopic bumps called papillae. Many are filiform papillae, which help the tongue grip food. Other types of papillae house sensors called taste buds that detect tastes in food. Fungiform papillae (pictured) detect the full range of tastes, while about ten big circumvallate papillae at the back of the tongue are more sensitive to bitter tastes.

Umami is from a Japanese word, translated as "pleasant savoury taste". It was scientifically indentified in 1908 by Kikunae Ikeda, a professor at Tokyo Imperial University.

Olives are often considered "an acquired taste", foods that are disliked at first but then liked after trying a few times.

Various parts of the tongue were thought to be exclusively responsible for different tastes. This zone was thought to detect salty tastes.

Sweet sensations are detected by the taste buds and recognized as enjoyable by the brain.

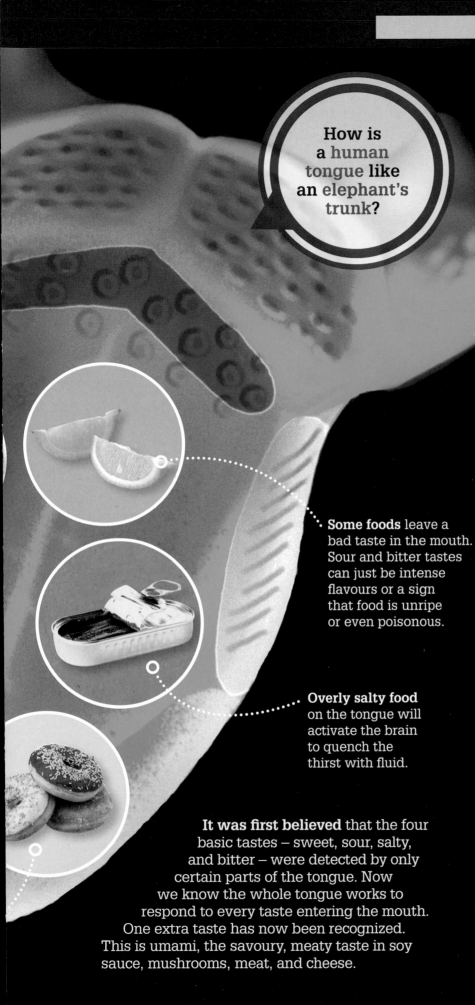

How is
a human
tongue like
an elephant's
trunk?

Some foods leave a bad taste in the mouth. Sour and bitter tastes can just be intense flavours or a sign that food is unripe or even poisonous.

Overly salty food on the tongue will activate the brain to quench the thirst with fluid.

It was first believed that the four basic tastes – sweet, sour, salty, and bitter – were detected by only certain parts of the tongue. Now we know the whole tongue works to respond to every taste entering the mouth. One extra taste has now been recognized. This is umami, the savoury, meaty taste in soy sauce, mushrooms, meat, and cheese.

FAST FACTS

80% OF THE FLAVOUR SENSATION
WE GET FROM FOOD COMES FROM ITS SMELL

The nose can detect more than one trillion different odours, but when it is blocked, food becomes almost flavourless. Try eating something while holding your nose shut. Food will be almost tasteless.

WOMEN'S SENSE OF SMELL IS STRONGER THAN MEN'S

Not only have women shown that they can smell better than men, but their sense of taste is stronger. Women are also better at finding the words to describe what it is they are smelling and tasting.

THE MOUTH HAS ONE MILLION TASTE RECEPTOR CELLS

There are up to 100 of these specialized cells in each of the taste buds. Tiny taste "hairs" attached to each receptor cell detect taste molecules dissolved in saliva. Receptor cells then send messages to the brain, which identifies tastes in food.

TRUE or FALSE? # Head lice like dirty hair

Head lice don't care about **bad hair days**. These critters aren't choosy. If your **crowning glory** is clean or dirty, these bad boys jump in and make themselves at home. But bring on the **chemical treatments** and the problem will soon be washed away!

Head lice pass quickly from head to head, so children at school are most at risk.

MICROSCOPIC MITES

You may not realize it but living in your eyelash follicles are microscopic mites like this one. They feed on dead skin cells and oily secretions from your scalp. They are too tiny to see and there's no way to get rid of these uninvited but harmless guests.

Each head louse has six clawed legs, which they use to grip hair as they bite into the scalp to feed on the blood.

FAST FACTS

9 M (30 FT)
7.3 M (24 FT)
5.5 M (18 FT)
3.7 M (12 FT)
1.8 M (6 FT)
0 M (0 FT)

IF THE AVERAGE MAN NEVER SHAVED HIS BEARD, IT WOULD GROW TO MORE THAN 9 M (30 FT) IN A LIFETIME

The longest beard on a man measured 1.83 m (6 ft) from the end of the chin to the tip of the beard. The longest beard on a woman measured 27.9 cm (11 in). Beard hair, like other types of hair, grows in phases. There is a growth phase and a resting phase before it falls out from its follicle to be replaced by a new hair.

Which natural hair colour is the rarest in the world?

ALEXANDER THE GREAT BANNED BEARDS

Alexander the Great (356–323 BCE) is always depicted as clean-shaven and he ordered his soldiers to shave, too. He believed that in combat, beards provided enemy soldiers with a "handle" to hold on to, giving them a military advantage.

Hair is the fastest growing tissue in the human body, apart from bone marrow. Made of a tough protein called keratin, hair keeps in heat and cushions against sudden impacts. About 100 hairs are lost from the scalp every day, though it is not enough to notice.

A female head louse produces about five eggs a day, and these are visible as tiny white specks on hair shafts near to the scalp. They take 7–10 days to hatch.

TRUE or FALSE?

TRUE or FALSE? You catch a **cold** from being **cold**

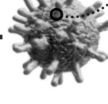

More than 200 different viruses can cause the common cold, with symptoms including sneezing, sore throats, and blocked noses.

While it is true that colds are more **common in winter** and cold air can create **runny noses**, this statement gets the **cold shoulder**. The only thing that causes a cold is a **cold virus**.

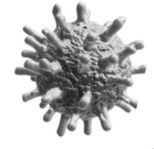

ANTIBIOTIC REVOLUTION

Antibiotics can help the body to fight infections. These wonder drugs target and kill specific bacteria, but they cannot cure a cold. This is because colds are caused by viruses, and antibiotics work only against bacteria.

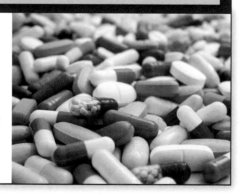

As the cold invaders advance, the nasal lining fights back by producing mucus – a sticky trap for catching viruses, dust, and pollen.

📊 FAST FACTS

IT IS POSSIBLE TO SNEEZE WITH YOUR EYES OPEN

The eyelids snap shut naturally during a sneeze, but if they are held open it is still possible to sneeze – and contrary to popular legend, your eyes won't pop out! It is believed that our eyes close as protection from the microorganisms and particles contained in the sneeze.

SNEEZES CAN REACH TOP SPEEDS OF 160 KPH (100 MPH)

It is the force and magnitude of the sneeze that allow germs to spread so quickly, infecting others wherever the water droplets land.

COMPUTER KEYBOARDS ARE DIRTIER THAN TOILET SEATS

Other household items such as remote controls, telephones, and door handles also contain more bacteria than the average toilet seat. As toilet seats tend to be disinfected, they are often one of the cleanest surfaces in the house.

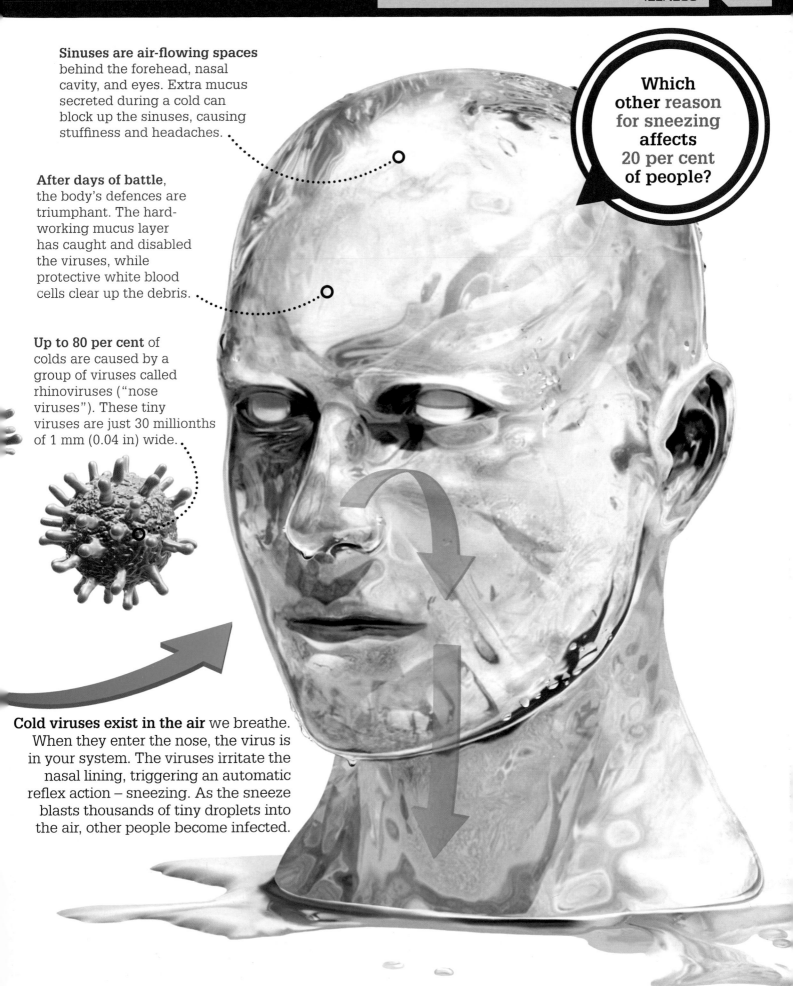

Sinuses are air-flowing spaces behind the forehead, nasal cavity, and eyes. Extra mucus secreted during a cold can block up the sinuses, causing stuffiness and headaches.

After days of battle, the body's defences are triumphant. The hard-working mucus layer has caught and disabled the viruses, while protective white blood cells clear up the debris.

Up to 80 per cent of colds are caused by a group of viruses called rhinoviruses ("nose viruses"). These tiny viruses are just 30 millionths of 1 mm (0.04 in) wide.

Which other reason for sneezing affects 20 per cent of people?

Cold viruses exist in the air we breathe. When they enter the nose, the virus is in your system. The viruses irritate the nasal lining, triggering an automatic reflex action – sneezing. As the sneeze blasts thousands of tiny droplets into the air, other people become infected.

TRUE or FALSE? Spinach makes you strong

Spinach **sweeps the board** at any food awards, leaving other vegetables **green with envy**. Though it packs a punch in the nutrition category, spinach is more of a **weakling** in the iron stakes. Instead, red meat and seafood **muscle in** to steal top prize for truly **cast-iron content**.

Fresh, leafy, organic spinach without any pesticide treatment is the best to eat.

SWEET TREAT

Made from cocoa beans, dark chocolate has multiple benefits. Its antioxidants protect against diseases and delay the signs of ageing, while flavonoids control blood-sugar levels. Phenylethylamine triggers the brain to release endorphins – chemicals responsible for feeling happy. So go on, treat yourself!

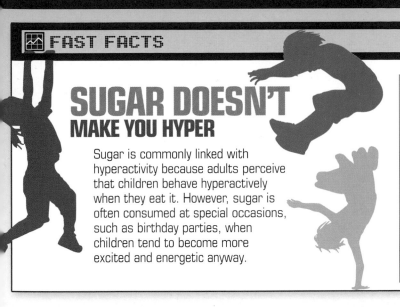

SUGAR DOESN'T
MAKE YOU HYPER

Sugar is commonly linked with hyperactivity because adults perceive that children behave hyperactively when they eat it. However, sugar is often consumed at special occasions, such as birthday parties, when children tend to become more excited and energetic anyway.

THE SMELL OF TOAST HAS BEEN PROVEN TO MAKE PEOPLE HAPPIER

Many people link the smell with happy memories of weekends and family. When memories are triggered by smell it is known as the "Proust effect". This can be used to help sell things. For example, when a house for sale smells of baking bread and fresh coffee, it can make potential buyers feel more at home.

Cooking spinach improves its health benefits, with just half a cup of cooked spinach providing three times the nutrition of one cup of raw spinach.

Which vitamin is a must-have for your bones?

Like other green vegetables, spinach has high levels of vitamin B_6, which helps the body make proteins and release energy.

An iron-rich diet is essential to stay strong, but spinach is average in terms of iron levels. However, spinach is crammed with vitamins and minerals. As a source of beta-carotene, spinach is a battler in the fight against serious disease. Its properties protect the heart, boost the skin, improve eye health, and keep the digestive system functioning.

TRUE or FALSE? We share 96% of DNA with chimps

There's **monkey business** going on at the **gene pool**. All living organisms came from the **same family tree** and that is why everything uses DNA to store its **genetic instructions**. Chimpanzees are our **closest relatives**, with almost identical genes.

Mouse - 75%

This primate is closest to humans because it shares 96% of the same DNA.

Chimpanzee - 96%

BACK TO THE START

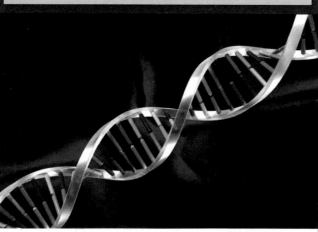

Each body cell contains long molecular strands of deoxyribonucleic acid (DNA) in a double-helix formation. Our DNA holds the instructions to build and operate a living human being. These instructions are written in code using combinations of four "letters".

Genetic testing companies can examine your DNA to trace your ancestors, creating personalized family trees. A much more mindboggling family tree comes from going back in time to find common ancestors with humans. All kinds of things share surprisingly large sequences of DNA with us, as shown here.

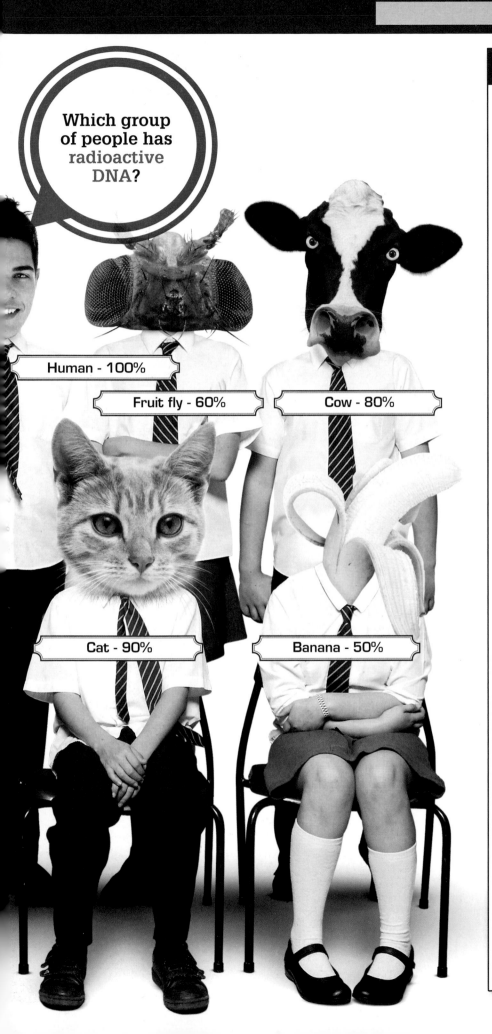

Which group of people has radioactive DNA?

Human - 100%

Fruit fly - 60%

Cow - 80%

Cat - 90%

Banana - 50%

TWO BROWN-EYED PARENTS CAN HAVE A BLUE-EYED CHILD

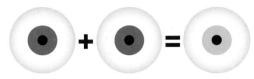

As long as both parents carry the gene for blue eyes, it is possible for them to have a blue-eyed child. Human eye colour is determined by multiple genes and the process is so complex that almost any parent-child combination can occur.

ALL HUMANS HAVE UNIQUE DNA – EVEN IDENTICAL TWINS

Almost all (99.9 per cent) of human DNA sequences are the same in every person. However, our genetic make-up is made of more than three billion letters, so the remaining 0.01 per cent leaves room for a great many differences. Identical twins begin life with the same DNA but as they grow, and letters are copied, in each twin different "typos" happen, meaning their DNA is not exactly the same.

ALL LIVING HUMANS CAN BE TRACED BACK TO ONE COMMON ANCESTOR IN AFRICA

"Mitochondrial Eve", who lived up to 200,000 years ago, was the most recent ancestor to all humans alive today if their ancestry is traced through the female line (mitochondrial). English naturalist Charles Darwin was the first to propose common descent of living organisms.

TRUE or FALSE? Your **ears** and **nose** keep **growing** as you age

Have you **heard** this one before? **Cartilage tissue** in the ears and nose **continues to grow** as you age. The earlobes also **elongate** as **gravity** pulls them downwards.

Saggy ears can be the result of the skin's elasticity losing its firmness.

LONGEST LIVING LADY

The world's oldest person was Jeanne Calment (1875–1997). The French cycling enthusiast died aged 122 years, 164 days. She claimed the secret to longevity was being calm and carefree.

The skin of older people is often wrinkled because the dermis produces far less collagen and elastin fibres that keep the skin of younger people firm and wrinkle-free.

The effects of time catch up with all of us eventually. While the ears and nose keep growing, the rest of the body starts slowing. Cells and tissue become worn out, and the skin thins and wrinkles. Eyesight and hearing both deteriorate.

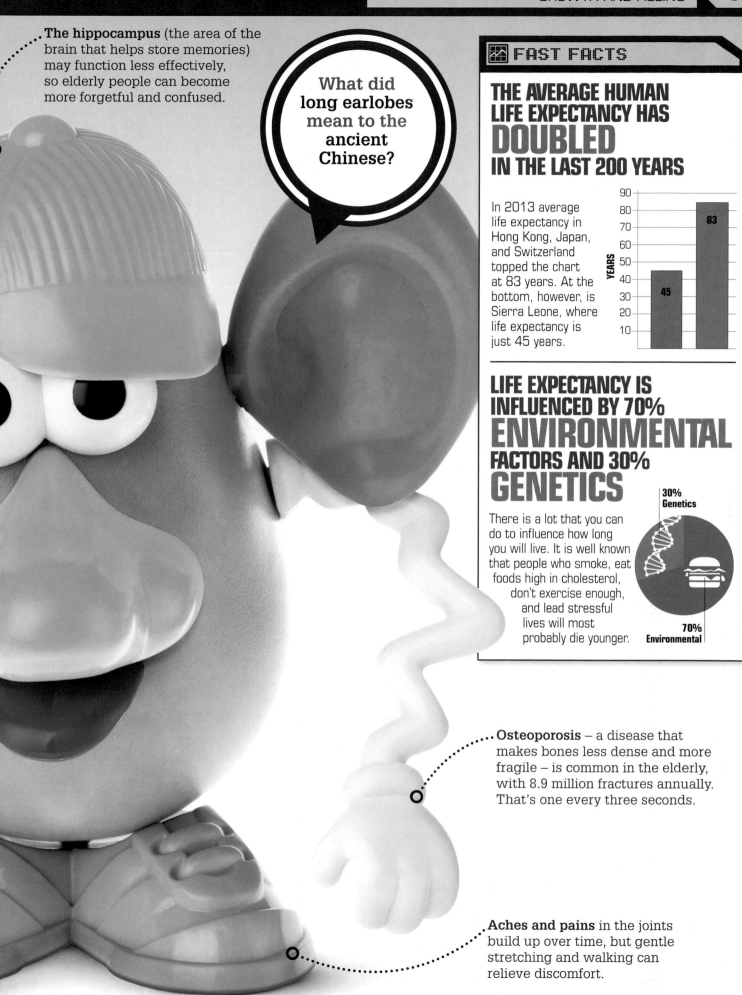

The hippocampus (the area of the brain that helps store memories) may function less effectively, so elderly people can become more forgetful and confused.

What did long earlobes mean to the ancient Chinese?

FAST FACTS

THE AVERAGE HUMAN LIFE EXPECTANCY HAS DOUBLED IN THE LAST 200 YEARS

In 2013 average life expectancy in Hong Kong, Japan, and Switzerland topped the chart at 83 years. At the bottom, however, is Sierra Leone, where life expectancy is just 45 years.

YEARS
90
80
70
60
50
40
30
20
10

45   83

LIFE EXPECTANCY IS INFLUENCED BY 70% ENVIRONMENTAL FACTORS AND 30% GENETICS

There is a lot that you can do to influence how long you will live. It is well known that people who smoke, eat foods high in cholesterol, don't exercise enough, and lead stressful lives will most probably die younger.

30% Genetics

70% Environmental

Osteoporosis – a disease that makes bones less dense and more fragile – is common in the elderly, with 8.9 million fractures annually. That's one every three seconds.

Aches and pains in the joints build up over time, but gentle stretching and walking can relieve discomfort.

Body talk

WOW THAT'S LONG!

The longest bone in the body, the femur (thigh bone) is one quarter of your height.

The **DIGESTIVE TRACT** is a **9 m** (30 ft) tube running from your mouth to your bottom. That's almost the length of a **school bus.**

If the **DNA** from **ONE CELL** was stretched out, it would be about **2 m** (6.5 ft) in length. That's about as tall as an adult man.

HANG ON A MINUTE

Every minute, you:

- produce **120 million** red blood cells in bone marrow

- shed about **40,000** skin cells

- make **180** tiny eye movements

- have **70** heartbeats

- take **20** breaths

- process **1,200 ml** (2.1 pints) of blood in your kidneys, making **1 ml** (0.002 pints) of urine

THE HARD STUFF

The **SMALLEST** bone in your body is the size of a grain of rice. It is called the **STIRRUP** and is one of three bones in the ear.

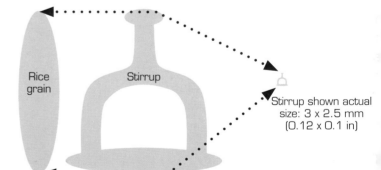

Rice grain

Stirrup

Stirrup shown actual size: 3 x 2.5 mm (0.12 x 0.1 in)

A fingernail would grow about **28 m** (90 ft) if it was never cut.

That's about the length of **four** elephants.

ON THE MOVE

Blood travels **19,000 km** **(12,000 miles)** every day. That's halfway around the world, or about the same as flying from the **North Pole to the South Pole.**

The fastest nerve signals can travel about **402 kph** (250 mph). That's faster than a peregrine falcon and a **Formula 1** racing car.

FORMULA 1 CAR	PEREGRINE FALCON	NERVE SIGNAL
386 kph	**389 kph**	**402 kph**
(240 mph)	(242 mph)	(250 mph)

You are born with **300** bones, but when you are fully grown, you have only **206.**

The enamel of your teeth is the **HARDEST** substance in the body. It has no living cells, so your body cannot repair it once it's damaged.

FEELING SLEEPY

A hormone called melatonin peaks at night to make people feel sleepy.

YOU SPEND ABOUT **ONE-THIRD** OF YOUR LIFE ASLEEP.

66.7%

Teenagers don't produce **melatonin** until 1am. This is much later than most adults, which may be why it's hard to get teenagers out of bed in the morning!

WATER IN THE BODY

At least **50%** of your body is water. But how much of each **organ** is water?

LIVER 86%

KIDNEYS 83%

BRAIN 80%

LUNGS 80%

HEART 73%

BONES 22%

Your feet have approximately **250,000** sweat glands. They can make **0.5 litres** (1 pint) of sweat each day.

Nature

A rich diversity of life exists on Earth. It is thought at least 8.7 million species share our planet, ranging from bacteria to mammals and algae to flowering plants. No wonder there are so many misconceptions about life on Earth. This walk on the wild side is a truth-seeking trek to set the records straight.

Artic terns create flight patterns in the sky at sunset over Iceland. Known as "sea swallows", these birds migrate to Antarctica to breed during the southern summer, avoiding the cold northern winter.

Birds are descended from dinosaurs

If a little bird told you our feathered **friends** are related to the great dinosaurs who roamed Earth **245–65 million years ago,** would you believe it? Recent **fossilized remains** discovered in **ancient rocks** have ruffled a few feathers. Birds are now known to be **descendents of dinosaurs with many shared characteristics.**

EXCEPTIONAL EVOLUTION

Evolution works in all kinds of interesting ways. Despite being a vulture, the palm-nut vulture eats mostly a vegetarian diet. The New Zealand kea (above) is a similar example. Instead of eating fruit and nuts like most parrots, the kea is an omnivore and will feed on fish, crabs, birds, and reptiles when plants are scarce.

A feathered species named *Archaeopteryx* (meaning "ancient wing") had wings the same basic shape as birds do today, so feathered wings probably first evolved for warmth and only later for flight.

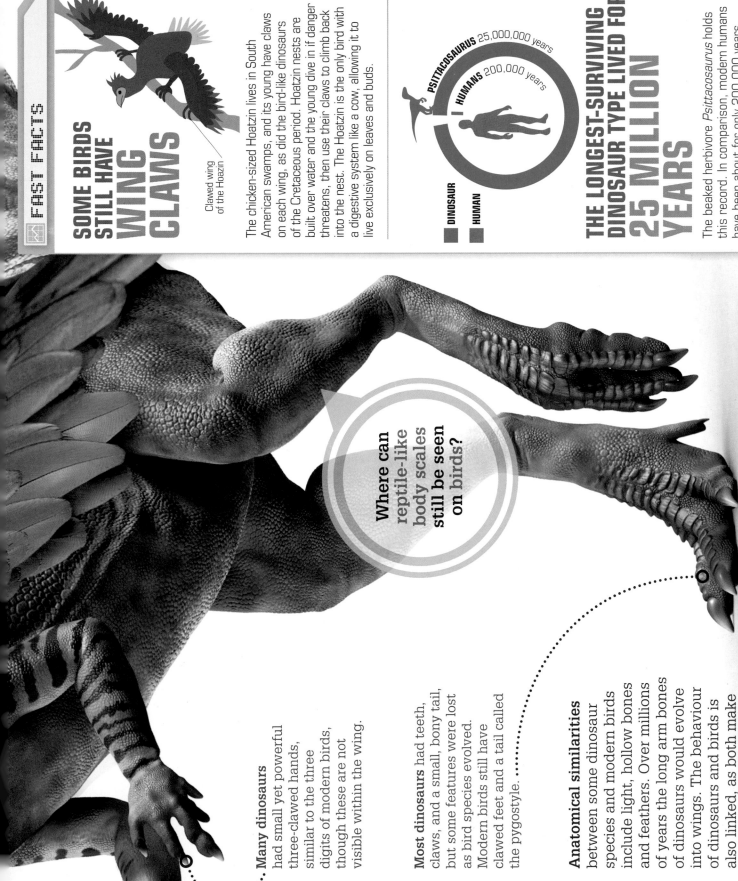

FAST FACTS

SOME BIRDS STILL HAVE WING CLAWS

Clawed wing of the Hoatzin

The chicken-sized Hoatzin lives in South American swamps, and its young have claws on each wing, as did the bird-like dinosaurs of the Cretaceous period. Hoatzin nests are built over water and the young dive in if danger threatens, then use their claws to climb back into the nest. The Hoatzin is the only bird with a digestive system like a cow, allowing it to live exclusively on leaves and buds.

PSITTACOSAURUS 25,000,000 years
HUMANS 200,000 years

DINOSAUR
HUMAN

THE LONGEST-SURVIVING DINOSAUR TYPE LIVED FOR 25 MILLION YEARS

The beaked herbivore *Psittacosaurus* holds this record. In comparison, modern humans have been about for only 200,000 years.

Where can reptile-like body scales still be seen on birds?

Many dinosaurs had small yet powerful three-clawed hands, similar to the three digits of modern birds, though these are not visible within the wing.

Most dinosaurs had teeth, claws, and a small, bony tail, but some features were lost as bird species evolved. Modern birds still have clawed feet and a tail called the pygostyle.

Anatomical similarities between some dinosaur species and modern birds include light, hollow bones and feathers. Over millions of years the long arm bones of dinosaurs would evolve into wings. The behaviour of dinosaurs and birds is also linked, as both make nests and lay eggs.

TRUE or FALSE? T-rex was the biggest dinosaur

Part of a vertebra from the backbone of a dinosaur called *Amphicoelias* was found more than a century ago. Its size suggested the species was a staggering 40–60 m (130–196 ft) long.

The tail lined with muscle acted as a counterbalance to the head and body when T-rex was in motion.

Tyrannosaurus rex may not have been the biggest dinosaur, but it was one of the biggest biters. Able to bite with about four times the strength of an alligator's jaws, this meat-muncher sealed the fate of its prey instantly. By ripping the skin apart, T-rex could feast on the juicy flesh underneath.

T-rex was 12 m (39 ft) in length.

Long, muscular legs and powerful thighs were built to run.

Great claws provided traction for stable movement

FAST FACTS

THE LARGEST FLYING ANIMAL WAS THE SIZE OF AN AEROPLANE

With a whopping wingspan of 11 m (36 ft), the huge pterosaur *Quetzalcoatlus* was about the size of the Spitfire aeroplane used in World War II. Despite its size, it weighed no more than 250 kg (550 lb).

THE BIGGEST DINOSAURS WERE AS HEAVY AS SIX FIRE ENGINES

Argentinosaurus, a massive sauropod from the Cretaceous period, was about 30 m (98 ft) long and weighed somewhere between 60 and 100 tonnes, as heavy as six fire engines.

The **poster boy predator** of the prehistoric period, *Tyrannosaurus rex* dominated the last age of the dinosaurs. But the "**tyrant lizard**" was surpassed in size by many **much bigger** species.

Forward-facing eyes provided binocular vision to launch attacks on prey.

Powerful jaws, lined with more than 60 spear-like teeth, were able to bite through solid bone.

When does a dog **sound exactly like** a T-rex?

Each strong arm had two or three claws.

Slim ankles suggest that T-rex could run quite fast.

FOSSILIZED FINDS

Part of the border between Utah and Colorado, USA, is now called Dinosaur National Monument. This region is home to a big collection of dinosaur fossils, with one sandstone wall housing 1,500 bones. These fossils tell us what we know about dinosaurs today.

TRUE or FALSE? Crocodiles **cry** when they eat **prey**

Beware the **crocodile smile**, and watch out when it weeps! Crocodiles **tear off lumps of food** and **swallow them whole**. Glands to keep the eyes moist are near their throats, so feeding **produces tears**. But don't offer a tissue unless you want to be next on the menu…

Without sweat glands, **how do crocodiles release heat?**

JESUS LIZARD

The basilisk lizard is at home in the trees of Central and South America. Known as the "Jesus lizard", this reptile is able to run across water, thanks to big fringed feet creating pockets of air around them. This generates forces sufficient to stay upright on water, a miraculous skill that comes in useful when escaping forest predators.

 **FAST FACTS**

A TURTLE'S HEART KEEPS BEATING LONG AFTER ITS DEATH

In many animals, the beating of the heart is controlled by the brain, but special nerve cells in the heart can keep it beating even if it has been removed from the body. Usually this phenomenon does not last long, but a turtle's heart can continue to beat for hours.

RATTLESNAKES CAN KILL EVEN AFTER THEY HAVE DIED

Don't think for a second that chopping off a rattlesnake's head will be the end of it – for that head can see, move, and bite with its deadly fangs up to an hour after the final blow!

One of the closest living relatives of dinosaurs, crocodiles are the most powerful reptiles. These skilled hunters can ambush, kill, and devour all kinds of prey. If a crocodile drowns a zebra, it can survive for months without needing to make another kill.

Stones are swallowed by crocodiles to help them grind up food inside their stomachs, and also act as ballast to stabilize them in the water.

A crocodile's tongue is connected to the roof of the mouth.

A range of fish, birds, and other creatures are eaten by crocodiles.

These reptiles can regrow a set of teeth to replace old or missing ones at least 40 times during their lives.

TRUE or FALSE? Elephants never forget

This is more than just mumbo jumbo. Elephants **recognize** old friends after long periods apart and **know the scents** of about 30 relatives. Grieving elephants **touch the skulls and tusks** of the deceased with their trunks and **return** to the site as if in mourning.

Elephants are sensitive and tactile, showing tenderness and concern when their babies are upset. They enjoy regular play time, which strengthens social bonds. As a form of greeting, two elephants may wrap their trunks together affectionately.

print safari pictures

must pack trunk

The trunk contains more than 100,000 muscles and the tip is dextrous enough to pick up a peanut.

CLEVER KANZI

Kanzi, a male bonobo, communicates with humans using lexigrams (symbols that represent words). He can also use tools, and even cook food over a campfire – showing a human-like ability to think and express himself.

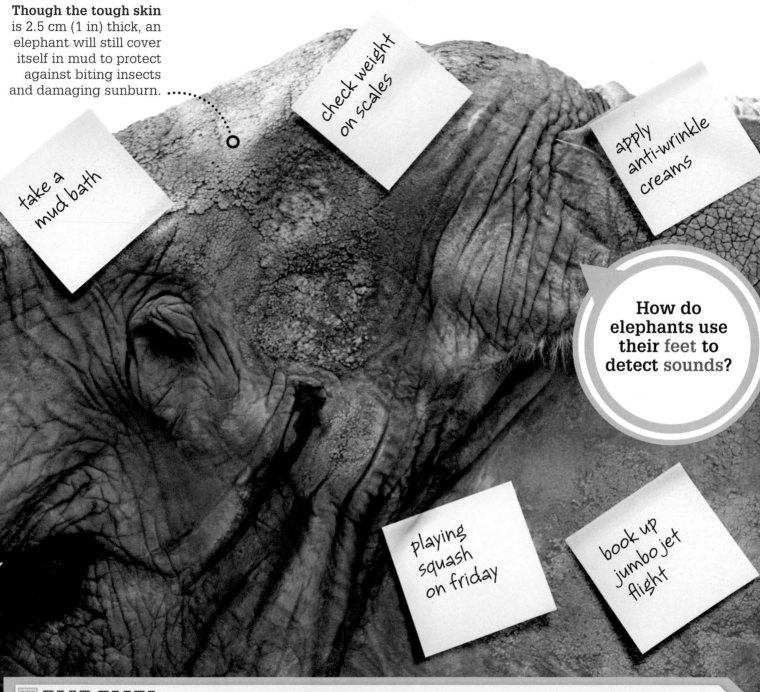

Though the tough skin is 2.5 cm (1 in) thick, an elephant will still cover itself in mud to protect against biting insects and damaging sunburn.

take a mud bath

check weight on scales

apply anti-wrinkle creams

How do elephants use their feet to detect sounds?

playing squash on friday

book up jumbo jet flight

📊 FAST FACTS

KOALAS SLEEP FOR UP TO 22 HOURS A DAY

These sleepyheads are diet-conscious. Koalas eat only eucalyptus leaves, and these tough, fibrous, and not very nutritious plants require a lot of energy to digest. Sleeping for most of the day helps koalas to conserve energy.

SOME ANIMALS DISCARD THEIR BODY PARTS

When threatened by a predator, some lizards will leave their tails to distract their attackers as they make a quick getaway. Stags often cast off their antlers after fighting over females, and snakes shed their skins when they outgrow the old one.

JAPANESE MACAQUES LOVE A HOT BATH

In 1963 the first Japanese macaque (a type of monkey) ventured into the hot water springs at the Jigokudani Monkey Park in Nagano, Japan. Soon, all the macaques were warming themselves in winter by bathing regularly, showing they learn by example.

TRUE or FALSE?

Camels store water in their humps

Please, don't **get the hump** if you thought this was true. A camel's hump is really a **huge lump of fat**. This is a food store, which allows the camel to **survive for long periods** in the desert.

A camel's nostrils trap and suck in the moisture in their breath so it is not lost.

Two rows of long eyelashes help to prevent sand entering the eyes during sandstorms.

Camels are resilient creatures, designed to cope with the difficulties of desert life. Their many adaptations include a long large intestine to ensure the maximum absorption of water in their food supply. When food or water is very scarce, fat inside the hump breaks down to give an energy boost.

FAST FACTS

SOME INSECTS SURVIVE BEING FROZEN SOLID FOR THE WINTER

The woolly bear caterpillar lives in cold regions, such as the Arctic. When the winter comes the caterpillar is frozen solid, causing its heart to stop beating. It is adapted to survive the cold and thaws once the ice melts in the spring.

STARFISH CAN CHANGE GENDER

The Astirina gibbosa starfish is born male, but changes into a female as it gets older. Other starfish change their gender according to the availability of food and mates.

CHIPMUNKS STORE FOOD IN THEIR CHEEKS

Chipmunks use this special ability to transport peanuts and other food items. They have fur-lined cheek pouches that expand and keep the food fresh, allowing them to carry it to their burrows for safekeeping.

EVOLUTIONARY ECHIDNA

Australia's echidna has multiple adaptations for feeding and self-defence. A long snout and sticky tongue help it reach into anthills to devour insects. Attackers are caught off guard when the spiny echidna curls up into a spiky ball.

How long does a camel take to drink 100 litres (26 gallons) of water?

Long legs allow the camel to move easily over long distances, and also elevate the body high above the sand, which is blazing hot.

The fat in a camel's hump, its narrow back, and thick coat all insulate the body against the Sun's scorching heat.

HELPING HUMANS

Occasionally shark attacks result in dolphins coming to aid the victims. Surfer Todd Endris was bitten by a shark in California, USA, in 2007. A pod of bottlenose dolphins circled him and helped him to shore. He says they saved his life.

The most fearsome predatory fish, the great white shark has a reputation as the ultimate marine monster. However, most attacks on humans are accidental, often occurring when sharks mistake surfboards on the surface for sealions and seals – their favourite food.

Great white sharks eat about 11 tonnes of food a year. They use and lose more than 1,000 teeth during their lifetime of at least 70 years.

TRUE OR FALSE?

Falling coconuts kill more people than sharks

Falling coconuts can kill, but it's an **urban legend** that they are more deadly than sharks. On average **eight people** are killed by sharks annually. **Ten times** more are killed by non-venomous insects, **30 times** more by dogs, and **60 times** more by hornets, wasps, or bees.

The average length of a great white shark is 4 m (13 ft), but one of the biggest ever caught was 6 m (20 ft) long, off Prince Edward Island, Canada, in 1993.

Which amazing sensory ability do sharks and tigers have in common?

FAST FACTS

BOX JELLYFISH ARE THE REAL MARINE KILLERS

Don't underestimate the most venomous creature on Earth, as it causes about 100 deaths per year. The venom attacks the heart, nervous system, and skin, with survivors still experiencing pain weeks after contact.

HIPPOPOTAMUSES ARE AFRICA'S MOST PROLIFIC KILLER CREATURES

Despite looking cuddly and kind, hippos have powerful jaws and large, sharp teeth. On top of this, they are fiercely aggressive if threatened and kill about 3,000 people a year.

HIPPOPOTAMUS
3,000 per year

CROCODILE
1,000 per year

ELEPHANT
500 per year

MOSQUITO BITES ARE ESTIMATED TO KILL TWO MILLION PEOPLE A YEAR

AREAS REPORTING DEATHS FROM MALARIA

Mosquitoes carry the Plasmodium parasite, and female mosquito bites transmit diseases to 700 million people annually. Of this number, two million die, mostly from malaria, a disease that attacks the blood.

TRUE or FALSE?

Chameleons change colour to suit their surroundings

If chameleons had wardrobes, they would switch outfits all day long. But their **changing appearance** is not always about **blending in**. **Light** and **temperature** affect chameleon colours, or they may just be **in the mood** for a change!

Which animals have striped skin as well as striped fur?

Science has shown that chameleons don't want to be part of a crowd. Blending in is beneficial only when resting or under attack. Simple environmental changes, such as different lighting or temperature, can alter their skin colour in just 20 seconds. Mood swings show the biggest change. An irritable, angry chameleon displays the brightest, most vibrant colours of all.

Males are more colourful than females, with most going from brown to green. They become more brightly coloured when frightened, courting, or defending their territories.

Chameleon eyes move independently and each can swivel nearly 180 degrees.

Skin layers below the outer skin have chromatophores, which contain colour pigments that expand and contract to alter skin colour.

MARVELLOUS MIMICS

Some creatures closely resemble another species in order to confuse and deter predators. This is called mimicry. One example is the locust borer, an insect that looks and sounds like a bee, though it does not have the capacity to sting!

FAST FACTS

NO TWO ZEBRAS HAVE THE SAME STRIPES

Each one has a unique set of stripes. When they group together, predators find it hard to target one in the sea of stripes. Also, stripes are a way to avoid being bitten by blood-sucking insects, which prefer solid colours.

THE ARCTIC FOX CHANGES COLOUR WITH THE SEASONS

In the winter, when everything is blanketed in snow, the Arctic fox has long, thick, white fur to blend in and keep warm. In spring, the fox moults, and is left with a shorter coat that is grey, brown, black, or blue.

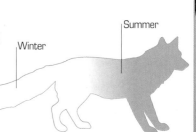

Winter

Summer

TRUE or FALSE? If scared, an **ostrich** will bury its **head** in the **sand**

This is a bird-brained idea. Ostriches do stick their heads in the sand, but **not through fear**. The world's **biggest bird** is **no chicken**. These **super sprinters** can escape danger by **fleeing at high speed** in the bushlands of their native Africa.

The long neck acts as a counterbalance for the weight of the body. Its length gives the eyes a good vantage point to spot and flee danger.

An ostrich eyeball is bigger than its brain.

MANY-TONGUED MIMIC

Northern mockingbirds are not only able to imitate the songs of many birds, but some can recreate other sounds, including a squeaking door, car alarm, and mewing cat. They are so good at imitating sounds that this skill is reflected in their scientific name, *Mimus polyglottos*, which means "many-tongued mimic".

The confusion over this myth comes from ostrich breeding behaviour. Once the female ostrich has laid her eggs, the male digs a hole in the sand where he moves the eggs for safekeeping. Each parent takes turns at sitting on the eggs and turning them over with their beaks during the day. As the eggs are turned over up to 0.9 m (3 ft) below the surface, it can look as though the ostrich has buried its head in the sand.

Ostriches stand up to 3 m (9 ft) in height.

An ostrich can weigh up to 180 kg (400 lb).

Ostriches have only two toes instead of the three or four toes of other bird species.

Ostrich eggs are the biggest of any bird — each one weighs up to 2.3 kg (5 lb), the same as 24 chicken eggs.

What speed is **the fastest** an ostrich can run in the wild?

FAST FACTS

AN ALBATROSS FLEW AROUND THE WORLD IN
46 DAYS

An albatross from South Georgia flew more than 22,000 km (13,670 miles) around the southern hemisphere in only 46 days. These amazing birds can glide on wind currents for hours at a time without flapping their wings and can even snooze while flying.

HUMMINGBIRDS ARE
ALWAYS HUNGRY

The energetic hummingbird has the fastest metabolism of any animal. It is so quick that despite the fact that it drinks more than its weight in nectar every day, it is always only a few hours from starving to death.

TRUE or FALSE? Mice like cheese

It is the food of choice for **cartoon mice**, but not for **real rodents**. While a hungry mouse will devour **virtually anything**, a choosy mouse opts for **fruit, grain, and seeds**.

RATTY REUNION

Contrary to popular belief, rats are sociable and affectionate creatures. A study in 2011 found that rats show empathy, going out of their way to help each other. When one rat was locked up, the other worked hard to free him. Each rat chose to release its companion even when food was offered as an alternative.

Mice are keen snackers, nibbling on different foods up to 20 times a day.

Whiskers help mice to navigate through small spaces and investigate their surroundings.

The country with the highest cheese consumption in the world per capita is Greece.

What is unusual about the incisor (front) teeth of mice?

Mice hide out near food sources. These accomplished climbers, jumpers, and swimmers navigate their way around homes and gardens easily. A recent study revealed that male mice sing love songs to females, but they are so high-pitched that we can't hear them. If things go well, a female house mouse can have up to 120 babies a year!

Mice love to explore, squeezing down small to fit through tiny gaps and biting clean through obstacles to keep moving.

FAST FACTS

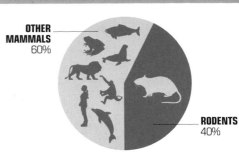

OTHER MAMMALS 60%

RODENTS 40%

ABOUT 40% OF ALL MAMMAL SPECIES ARE RODENTS

Rodents are possibly the most successful group of animals of all time, as they have survived for about 160 million years and remain abundant today.

THE ROMANS THOUGHT WHITE RATS WERE LUCKY

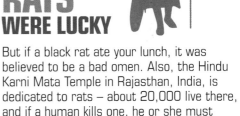

But if a black rat ate your lunch, it was believed to be a bad omen. Also, the Hindu Karni Mata Temple in Rajasthan, India, is dedicated to rats – about 20,000 live there, and if a human kills one, he or she must replace it with a solid gold statue of a rat.

THE LONGEST RAT IS THE SIZE OF A CAT

The Bosavi woolly rat was discovered as a television crew shot a documentary about Mount Bosavi, an extinct volcano in Papua New Guinea. At about 82 cm (32 in) long, it is a bit longer than the average domestic cat, which is 76.2 cm (30 in) long.

TRUE or FALSE? Bees **die** when they **sting** you

Honey bees **sting you and die**, but wasps can sting **again and again**. Confusion over the two types of stinger can cause **a bee in the bonnet** for some. To spot the difference if there's a buzz going on in your garden, bees are generally the **fatter**, **laid-back** ones, while wasps are **thinner but much angrier**!

Honey bees use sight and smell to locate flowers and find nectar.

BEE THERAPY

Some alternative therapists believe bee venom can help those suffering with diseases such as arthritis or multiple sclerosis. The affected area is deliberately stung to reduce pain and swelling. This treatment must follow doctor's advice because bee venom can cause anaphylactic shock, leading to sudden death, in a minority of allergic people.

Worker honey bees undertake various tasks, depending on their age and the requirements of the colony.

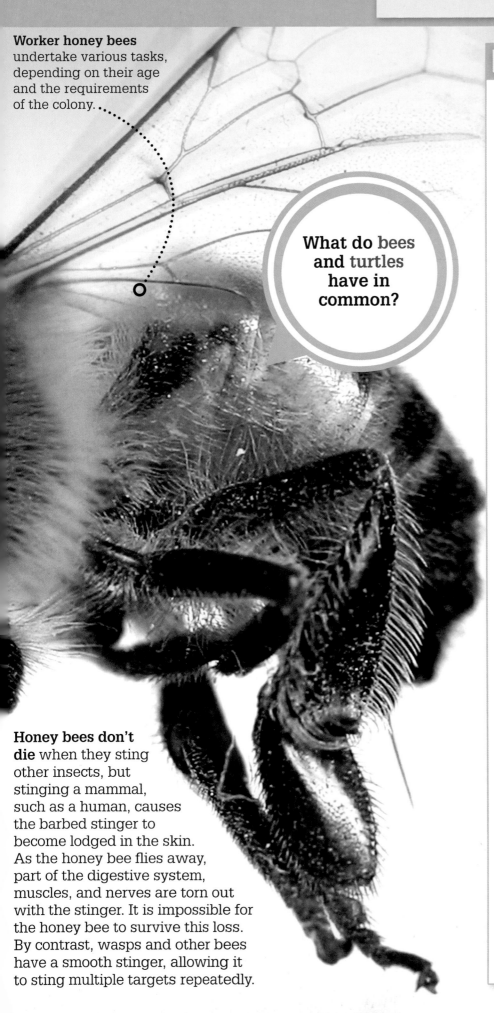

What do bees and turtles have in common?

Honey bees don't die when they sting other insects, but stinging a mammal, such as a human, causes the barbed stinger to become lodged in the skin. As the honey bee flies away, part of the digestive system, muscles, and nerves are torn out with the stinger. It is impossible for the honey bee to survive this loss. By contrast, wasps and other bees have a smooth stinger, allowing it to sting multiple targets repeatedly.

FAST FACTS

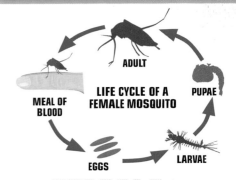

LIFE CYCLE OF A FEMALE MOSQUITO

ADULT

PUPAE

MEAL OF BLOOD

EGGS   LARVAE

ONLY FEMALE MOSQUITOES BITE

Female mosquitoes need nutrients from blood to produce eggs. Males prefer flower nectar because they don't make eggs. Once the females have laid their eggs, they die.

FIRE ANTS COORDINATE THEIR

BITE

WHEN THREATENED

Nobody quite knows how they do it, but if you bump into a fire ant nest, the counter-attack by the ants is organized so that all the ants will bite you at once. The effect is what gives the ants their name as it feels like being on fire. Ouch!

RATING	INSECTS
1.0	Southern fire ant (*Solenopsis xyloni*)
2.0	Honey bee, Africanized bee, bumble-bee, yellow-jacket ("common wasp")
3.0	Velvet ant, paper wasp
4.0	Tarantula hawk (*Pepsis wasp*)
4+	Bullet ant (*Paraponera clavata*)

THE STARR STING PAIN SCALE RANKS STINGS FROM ONE TO FOUR

Created by insect specialist Christopher Starr, this scale describes the pain of stings from bees, wasps, and ants. The bullet ant is the king of the stingers – its name says it all.

TRUE or FALSE? Goldfish have three-second memories

Goldfish are more gifted than people think. Studies have found them to be **fast learners** and **punctual timekeepers**, with the ability to remember colours, music, and other cues months later, **sinking this myth** to the bottom of the goldfish bowl.

How do goldfish save the lives of people?

SALMON SWIMMERS

Adult salmon nearly always return to the river in which they spent their early life to breed. Once close to home, these speedy swimmers detect minerals in the water and trace them to their birthplace where they go to lay eggs. Tagged salmon swam almost 3,220 km (2,000 miles) in 60 days through the Yukon River in Canada and Alaska.

Goldfish are the world's most popular pet fish.

Light is necessary for goldfish to produce orange pigmentation, otherwise they would go paler in the dark.

Researchers have played the brain game with goldfish, finding that they have a memory span of between three and five months. Taught to fetch balls, push levers, solve mazes, and limbo under bars, this multi-skilled marine life also enjoys routine, recognizing accurately when their daily feeding time will be.

FAST FACTS

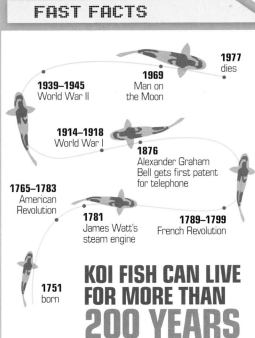

1977 dies

1969 Man on the Moon

1939–1945 World War II

1914–1918 World War I

1876 Alexander Graham Bell gets first patent for telephone

1765–1783 American Revolution

1781 James Watt's steam engine

1789–1799 French Revolution

1751 born

KOI FISH CAN LIVE FOR MORE THAN 200 YEARS

Like a tree, the age of a fish can be guessed by counting growth rings on its scales. Most koi fish die at about 50 years old, but legend has it that the oldest koi fish, called Hanako (meaning "flower maid"), was 226 years old when she died in 1977.

SOME LIPSTICKS CONTAIN FISH SCALES

Pearl essence (or pearlescence) is a silvery substance that is found in fish scales and used in lipsticks and nail polishes to give a shimmery effect. The scales are one of the many by-products from the commercial fish processing industry and are primarily obtained from herring. Synthetic versions of pearl essence have also been developed.

TRUE or FALSE? A **cockroach** can **live for three days** without its **head**

Surviving the **extinction of the dinosaurs**, these **hardcore critters** take toughness to the next level. They can live **without air** for 45 minutes and **without their heads** for at least three days. Be afraid, be very afraid!

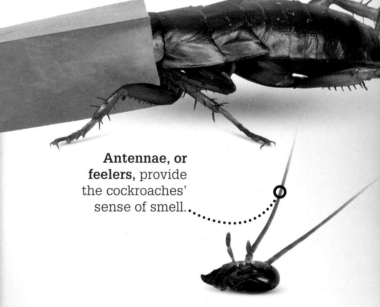

Antennae, or **feelers**, provide the cockroaches' sense of smell.

BUTTERFLY BRAIN

Developments in CT scanning have allowed scientists to study caterpillars during their metamorphosis into butterflies. They found that adult butterflies remembered things that happened to them while they were caterpillars. In a series of tests, butterflies reacted to bad smells in the same way they did as caterpillars, proving they remembered them.

The oldest fossil from a cockroach-like insect dates back to 315 million years ago. These super-strong miracles of nature can go for at least a month without food or water. They breed like wildfire and strike fear in people's hearts in the event of a home infestation. But very few species of cockroach live in cities. Most dwell in forests and caves a long way from civilization.

FAST FACTS

9 METRES equivalent to about 5 average people

9 M (29.5 FT)
7.3 M (24 FT)
5.5 M (18 FT)
3.7 M (12 FT)
1.8 M (6 FT)

TERMITE MOUNDS CAN REACH 9 M (29.5 FT) IN HEIGHT

The master builders of the insect world create their towering homes from a mixture of wood, soil, mud, saliva, and poo. Termites use openings at the base of the mound to enter and exit the nest, while workers add new tunnels and repair damage.

CANADA

USA

MEXICO

SOME MONARCH BUTTERFLIES FLY 2,800 KM (1,750 MILES) IN THEIR LIFETIME

Flying south to Mexico, some monarch butterflies travel far to escape cold weather. As well as being great fliers, they use special sensory organs on their feet and heads to identify their favourite plant, milkweed. They live for up to eight months.

There are 4,600 named species of cockroach.

These scavengers eat virtually anything to survive.

Could cockroaches survive a nuclear explosion?

Their six legs carry them at top speeds of 1.5 m/s (3.4 mph).

TRUE or FALSE? We swallow eight spiders a year in our sleep

This thought is a **nightmare** for those suffering with **arachnophobia** (fear of spiders), but it is nothing more than a **tangled web** of twaddle. The possibility of this situation ever happening is **highly unlikely**, and there are **no examples** in scientific or medical records.

WONDER WEBS

In 2012 scientists used computer simulations to find out how well spiderwebs withstood a range of stresses. Some could even survive hurricane-force winds! This super-strength helps the web stay intact when prey is trapped within it.

Common house spiders trap flies and other bugs in their webs before rushing out to consume them.

The leg span of a Goliath bird-eating spider is about the same size as a dinner plate.

Jumping spiders have eight eyes and can leap up to 50 times their own body length.

FAST FACTS

THE DIVING BELL SPIDER CAN STAY UNDERWATER FOR 24 HOURS

The only spider known to live entirely underwater, the diving bell spider weaves a silk container to trap air on the surface, which it then breathes through when underwater. Their supply usually lasts a day.

SPIDERWEBS CAN SPAN RIVERS

The largest spiderweb crafted by a single spider measured 25 m (82 ft). It was made by a Darwin's bark spider in 2010 and crossed a river in Andasibe-Mantadia National Park on the island of Madagascar.

SOME SPIDERS ARE PETROL HEADS

The yellow sac spider likes the smell of petrol so much that it builds webs in car engines. Over time the webs could cause blockage and build up of pressure. In 2014 Mazda recalled 42,000 cars over fears the webs could clog up fuel tanks, causing fires.

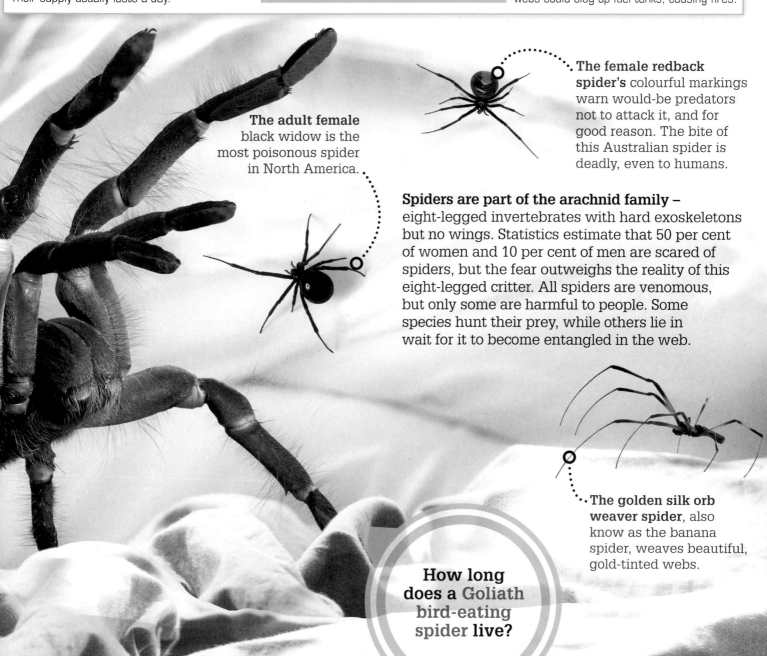

The adult female black widow is the most poisonous spider in North America.

The female redback spider's colourful markings warn would-be predators not to attack it, and for good reason. The bite of this Australian spider is deadly, even to humans.

Spiders are part of the arachnid family – eight-legged invertebrates with hard exoskeletons but no wings. Statistics estimate that 50 per cent of women and 10 per cent of men are scared of spiders, but the fear outweighs the reality of this eight-legged critter. All spiders are venomous, but only some are harmful to people. Some species hunt their prey, while others lie in wait for it to become entangled in the web.

The golden silk orb weaver spider, also know as the banana spider, weaves beautiful, gold-tinted webs.

How long does a Goliath bird-eating spider live?

TRUE or **FALSE?** Sunflowers follow the Sun across the sky

These devoted Sun worshippers soak up the rays in a process called **heliotropism**. Looking **east at dawn**, the flower heads track the Sun's path all day and **face west by dusk**.

A sunflower consists of more than 1,000 individual flowers joined together at the head.

FAST FACTS

TULIPS WERE WORTH **MORE THAN GOLD**

At least in 17th-century Netherlands, that is. The craze for the flower, introduced from Asia, led to bulbs being sold for more than 20 times the average annual wage at the height of "tulip mania".

BROCCOLI IS A **FLOWER**

Well, the bit you eat is. The green head of a broccoli plant will open into yellow flowers if left to grow. This is why they are called florets – they are little flowers that make up a flower head.

The green parts of sunflowers convert the energy from sunlight into sugar to help their rapid growth. This process is called photosynthesis. The tallest sunflower on record towered more than 8 m (27 ft).

One of the fastest growing plants, sunflowers may reach 2.5 m (8 ft) in just six months.

FLORAL STENCH

The rafflesia, or corpse flower, never comes up smelling of roses. Instead it blooms stinking of rotten flesh – hence its name – to attract insects, particularly flies. It dies a week later. Growing in the Indonesian rainforests, it is the world's largest flower and one of the rarest.

The petals of which flower can be **deadly to cats?**

TRUE or FALSE? A tomato is a fruit

Never **cherry-picked** for the fruit bowl, the tomato has spent its **salad days** with the green vegetables. But, by definition, a tomato is a fruit because it contains **the ovary** and **seeds** of a **flowering plant**.

Scientific studies have found that smelling or eating oranges improves people's moods.

Raspberries belong to the rose family.

Blueberries consist of more healthy antioxidants than any other fruit or vegetable.

Grapes have been used to make wine since about 5000 BCE.

More than 100 billion bananas are eaten annually worldwide.

FIVE-A-DAY FABLE

In 2011 scientific studies of more than 300,000 Europeans found that eating five portions of fruit and vegetables a day does not guarantee long life. Fruit and vegetables cannot prevent diseases unless combined with a healthy lifestyle and regular exercise.

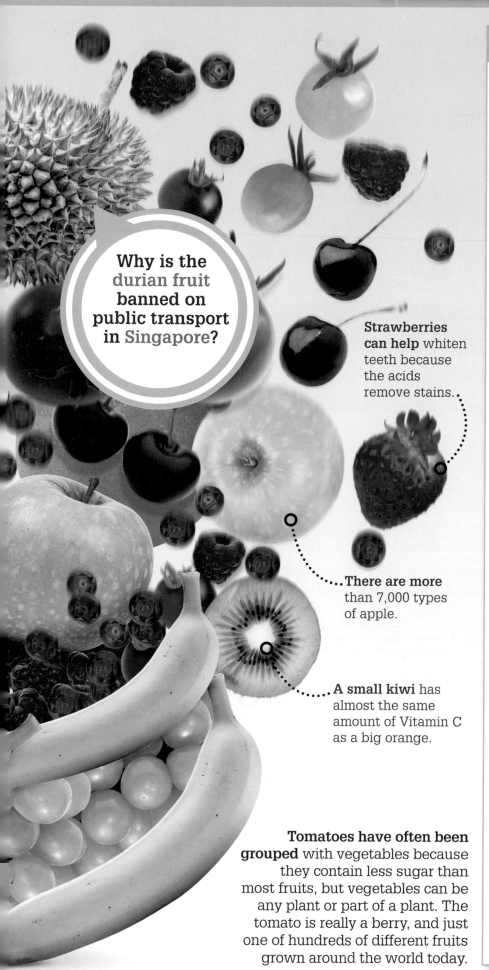

Why is the durian fruit banned on public transport in Singapore?

Strawberries can help whiten teeth because the acids remove stains.

There are more than 7,000 types of apple.

A small kiwi has almost the same amount of Vitamin C as a big orange.

Tomatoes have often been grouped with vegetables because they contain less sugar than most fruits, but vegetables can be any plant or part of a plant. The tomato is really a berry, and just one of hundreds of different fruits grown around the world today.

FAST FACTS

TWO CANTALOUPE MELONS SOLD FOR £12,000 ($23,500)

Auctioned in Japan in 2008, these two Yubari King cantaloupes are a luxury fruit, and were probably given as a gift. The town of Yubari produces a small number of these every year, which is why the demand (and the price!) is high.

PEANUTS ARE FRUIT

Nuts are large seeds with a hard shell. But for some, such as peanuts, almonds, hazelnuts, and chestnuts, the shell is in fact a fruit that is tough and fibrous rather than soft and juicy.

HELICOPTERS ARE USED TO DRY CHERRIES

When cherries absorb rain water they are prone to splitting because their skin cannot stretch. To prevent the cherries being ruined, helicopters fly over the trees to blow off the water and dry the fruit – just like a giant hair dryer!

Second nature

LIVING SPECIES

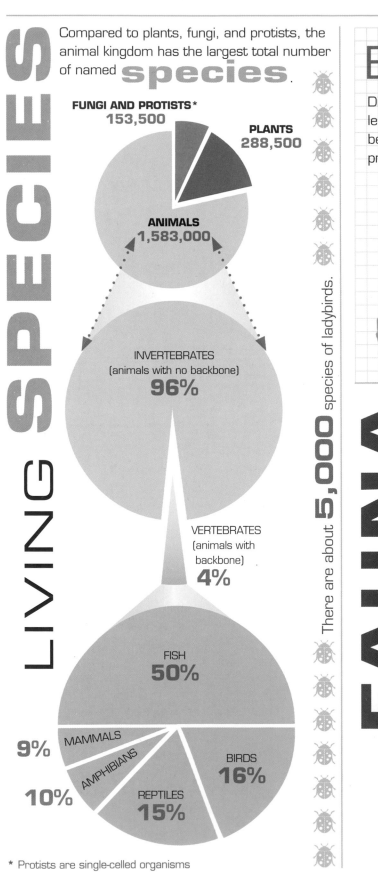

Compared to plants, fungi, and protists, the animal kingdom has the largest total number of named **species**.

FUNGI AND PROTISTS*
153,500

PLANTS
288,500

ANIMALS
1,583,000

INVERTEBRATES
(animals with no backbone)
96%

VERTEBRATES
(animals with backbone)
4%

FISH
50%

9% MAMMALS

AMPHIBIANS

BIRDS
16%

10%

REPTILES
15%

* Protists are single-celled organisms

There are about **5,000** species of ladybirds.

BED TIME

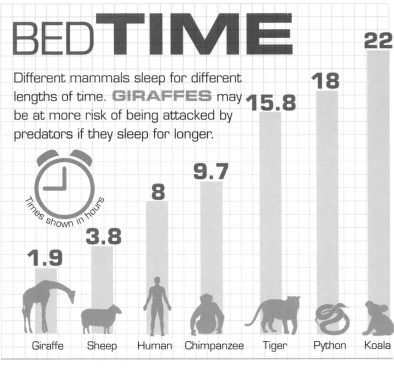

Different mammals sleep for different lengths of time. **GIRAFFES** may be at more risk of being attacked by predators if they sleep for longer.

Times shown in hours

Giraffe	Sheep	Human	Chimpanzee	Tiger	Python	Koala
1.9	3.8	8	9.7	15.8	18	22

FATAL FAUNA

Some animals can **kill people.** Here are the top killers per year:

MOSQUITOES
2,000,000

SNAKES
50,000

SCORPIONS
5,000

HIPPOPOTAMUSES
3,000

CROCODILES
1,000

JELLYFISH
180

SHARKS
8

LOUD SOUNDS OF THE *ANIMAL KINGDOM*

Animals that can be heard over a long distance:

BLUE WHALE'S SONG = 800 KM (500 MILES)

ELEPHANT'S STOMPS = 10 KM (6 MILES)

LION'S ROAR = UP TO 8 KM (5 MILES)

A **PISTOL SHRIMP** SNAPS ONE CLAW SHUT TO CREATE A BUBBLE THAT BURSTS **AT 200 DECIBELS** – LOUD ENOUGH TO STUN PREY.

ANIMAL YOUNG CAUGHT OUT

Chicken egg*

A VERVAIN HUMMINGBIRD EGG IS THE SIZE OF A **PEA**, ABOUT ONE-SIXTH THE HEIGHT OF A CHICKEN'S EGG.

Vervain hummingbird egg*

* both eggs shown actual size

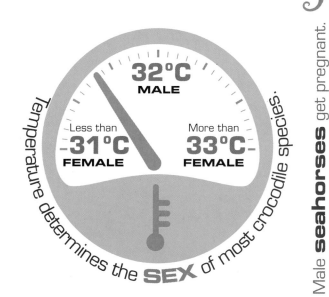

32°C MALE

Less than **-31°C FEMALE**

More than **33°C FEMALE**

Temperature determines the **SEX** of most crocodile species.

Male **seahorses** get pregnant.

There are more tigers held in captivity in the USA **(5,000)**

than there are in the wild in Asia. **(3,200)**.

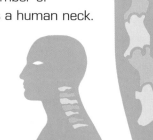

BODY PARTS

Octopuses have **THREE** hearts and jellyfish don't have a heart at all.

Giant squid can grow up to **15 m** (49 ft) long. That's about the same length as a small jet aeroplane.

Although a giraffe's neck is at least **1.5 m** (5 ft) tall, it contains the same number of vertebrae as a human neck.

Giant squid

Lear Jet 25D

15 m (49 ft)

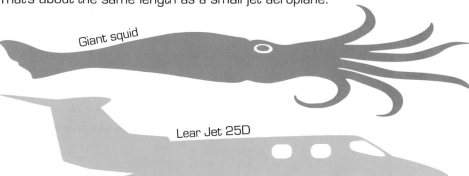

Science and technology

With brainboggling basics, innovative inventions, technological triumphs, and modern marvels, it's easy to become blinded by science. Misconceptions and misunderstandings abound, so it's time to get back on the same wavelength.

A US navy jet is caught on camera breaking the sound barrier of 344 m/s (1,130 ft/s). The aircraft leaves a huge, white vapour cloud in its wake, called a "shock collar".

TRUE or FALSE?

You can't boil water on top of a mountain

Forget enjoying a brew with a view. Water **does boil** at the top of a mountain, but at a **much lower temperature**. This is because **air pressure** is much **lower at altitude**. As a result, the water isn't hot enough and **lukewarm liquid** is no one's cup of tea.

Cooking in warm water takes much longer, so at very high altitudes, mountaineers sometimes use pressure cookers to make up for the low atmospheric pressure.

Which country drinks the most tea per person?

SALTY SEA

Seawater is more dense than freshwater because it has salt dissolved in it. The Dead Sea contains so much salt that it is denser than the human body. This is why bathers float on the surface.

Water evaporates (turns into vapour) all the time. The rate of evaporation increases with temperature. Water boils when vapour is produced quickly enough to exert the same pressure outwards as atmospheric pressure. As atmospheric pressure decreases with altitude, water boils at a lower temperature at the top of mountains, such as the Matterhorn, shown here.

Water is the only substance that occurs naturally on Earth as a solid (ice), liquid, and a gas (water vapour).

°C °F

°C	°F
50	120
40	100
30	80
20	60
10	40
0	32
10	20
20	0
30	20

FAST FACTS

A TAP DRIPPING ONCE A SECOND WASTES ENOUGH WATER TO FILL 100 BATHS

That's 10,000 litres (2,200 gallons) each year, and it shows why small changes can make a big difference when it comes to saving water. Two-thirds of water used in the home is used in the bathroom, and this is spread between flushing toilets, showering, and bathing.

MOST OF THE WORLD'S WATER SUPPLY IS USED FOR AGRICULTURE

DOMESTIC 8% **INDUSTRY 22%** **AGRICULTURE 70%**

Water usage around the world varies considerably. In Africa, agriculture uses 88 per cent of all water, while in Europe most water is used in industry.

WATER EXPANDS AS IT FREEZES

Unlike nearly all other substances, water expands as it cools from 4°C (39°F) to 0°C (32°F). Ice takes up 9 per cent more space than the same amount of cold water. This is why water pipes can burst on cold days.

TRUE or FALSE?

All light travels at the same speed

Fasten your seatbelts! Light travels **faster in a vacuum** (an area without matter) than anything in the Universe, at a speed of about 300,000 km/sec (186,000 miles/sec). But wherever light **passes through matter**, such as air, water, or glass, it **slows down**, stopping this myth in its tracks.

FAST FACTS

NASA'S X-43 SCRAMJET CAN FLY FROM NEW YORK TO LOS ANGELES IN 20 MINUTES

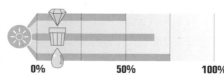

That's 0.000405 per cent of the speed of light! At approximately 11,000 km/h (7,000 mph), this is the fastest aircraft in history. It would take six hours for a normal passenger plane to make this journey.

WATER SLOWS THE SPEED OF LIGHT TO 75% OF ITS TOP SPEED IN A VACUUM

0%   50%   100%

Glass slows it to 66% and diamonds slow it to 50%. The molecules in these materials are so tightly packed that the light bumps into many molecules along the way, which means it takes longer to get from A to B.

AT THE SPEED OF LIGHT, YOU COULD CIRCLE THE EQUATOR 7.5 TIMES IN A SECOND

According to relativity, the speed of light is nature's ultimate speed limit – and only things with no mass, such as light, can ever travel that fast. To get *you* to light speed would require an infinite amount of energy.

Light can travel through a vacuum at breakneck speed because there is nothing to slow it down. If any matter is present, light interacts with it, and this slows it down. Light travels at different speeds in different materials – and if it moves from one to another at an angle, the light changes direction – this is why light bends when it passes through a glass lens, for example.

The presence of air slows down light waves.

Different colours are produced by different wavelengths of light. Red light travels very slightly faster through air or glass than blue light.

CALCULATIONS BY CANDLELIGHT

The intensity (brightness) of light is measured using a unit called a candela. It was originally based on the amount of light emanating from a single candle. A typical lightning flash produces light with an intensity of about eight trillion times that of a candle.

Which country uses the most light, based on electricity per capita?

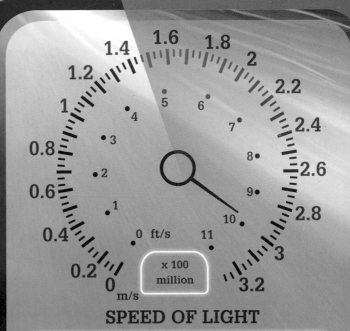

x 100 million

0 ft/s

SPEED OF LIGHT

299,792,458 m/s
983,571,056 ft/s

TRUE or FALSE?

An opera singer can shatter glass

Italian opera singer Enrico Caruso claimed his **high notes** could **shatter champagne flutes.** He was right — ear-piercing tones have been known to break glass. **A powerful voice** producing a **very loud, pure tone** at a **perfect pitch** can break a wine glass. **Smash!** You'd be left picking up the pieces.

SONIC BOOM

Speedy sound travels through air at 344 m/s (1,130 ft/s). Some things move faster still, breaking the sound barrier and creating a shock wave called a sonic boom. The crack of a whip is a sonic boom caused by part of the whip moving faster than the speed of sound.

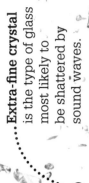

Extra-fine crystal is the type of glass most likely to be shattered by sound waves.

Glass has a natural resonant frequency — the speed it will vibrate when knocked by someone or disturbed by a sound wave. If a professional sings at the right pitch and volume to vibrate the air particles around the glass at its precise resonant frequency, the glass will vibrate. Raising the volume of singing can result in the glass breaking altogether.

Wine glasses are best candidates because their tubular shape produces a ringing sound when chinked.

The singer's vocal displaces surrounding air particles, sending them towards the glass at speed.

Why should you avoid whistling at the end of an opera?

FAST FACTS

SOUNDS ABOVE 85 DB CAN DAMAGE YOUR HEARING

Sound intensity is measured in decibels (dB). The louder the noise, the more decibels it racks up. Listening to sounds above 85 dB for long periods can hurt your ears, while sounds louder than 120 dB are painful.

NOISY RESTAURANT (80 dB)

ROCK CONCERT (100 dB)

AIRPLANE TAKE-OFF (130 dB)

NEARBY BLUE WHALE (180 dB)

NEARBY ROCKET LAUNCH (200 dB)

EPICENTRE OF A BIG EARTHQUAKE (300 dB)

SOUND TRAVELS ABOUT FOUR TIMES FASTER IN WATER THAN IN AIR

WATER

This is because water molecules in a liquid are much closer together than those in a gas, so it takes less time for the sound waves to pass through.

TRUE or FALSE? A rainbow has seven colours

All children know the **colours of the rainbow**, but the reality is not as black and white as **seven distinct colours**. Reflecting sunlight off water droplets, a rainbow **bounces back every wavelength** from infrared to ultraviolet, with **colours** running into **millions of kaleidoscopic shades**.

DEEP BLUE SEA

The sea isn't blue because it reflects the blue sky. An object looks a certain colour because it absorbs some wavelengths of light and reflects others. We see only the reflected ones. Seawater absorbs all colours except blue, so we see only the reflected blue wavelengths.

It is impossible to reach the end of a rainbow – as you move and your perspective changes, the rainbow moves, too.

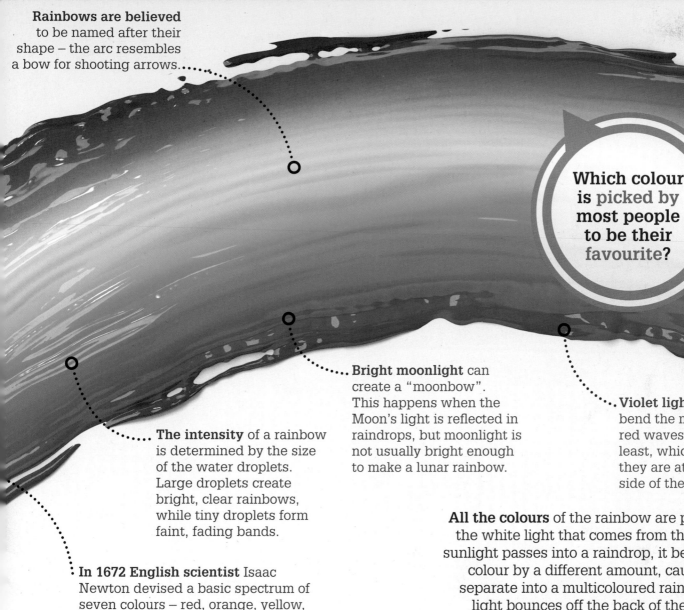

Rainbows are believed to be named after their shape – the arc resembles a bow for shooting arrows.

Which colour is picked by most people to be their favourite?

The intensity of a rainbow is determined by the size of the water droplets. Large droplets create bright, clear rainbows, while tiny droplets form faint, fading bands.

Bright moonlight can create a "moonbow". This happens when the Moon's light is reflected in raindrops, but moonlight is not usually bright enough to make a lunar rainbow.

Violet light waves bend the most and red waves bend the least, which is why they are at each side of the rainbow.

In 1672 English scientist Isaac Newton devised a basic spectrum of seven colours – red, orange, yellow, green, blue, indigo, and violet.

All the colours of the rainbow are present in the white light that comes from the Sun. As sunlight passes into a raindrop, it bends each colour by a different amount, causing it to separate into a multicoloured rainbow. The light bounces off the back of the raindrop and bends again as it exits the front.

📊 FAST FACTS

CHROMOPHOBIA
IS THE IRRATIONAL FEAR OF COLOURS

Fear of a certain colour can occur when a person experiences an extremely negative event associated with a particular colour. Symptoms may include any of the signs of anxiety such as heart palpitations, chest pain, or shortness of breath.

BEES CAN SEE COLOURS THAT HUMANS CAN'T

WHAT A HUMAN SEES　　　　**WHAT A BEE SEES**

Bees can see on the Ultraviolet (UV) spectrum, but this range is invisible to the naked human eye. Using special devices, scientists have discovered that the coloured world these insects see guides them to target "landing strips" where they feed on nectar.

COLOUR WHEEL

An artist's colour wheel shows how different coloured pigments mix together. Any colour can be made by mixing the "primary colours" – red, yellow, and blue – in different proportions. Any two primary colours mixed together produce the "secondary colours".

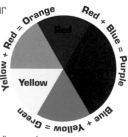

A coin dropped from a tall building can kill

Being **showered with money** sounds good in theory, but getting struck by a falling coin is said **to be fatal**. The truth is a falling coin is small and flat, with its speed **limited by air resistance.** Dropping one from a great height will **sting the skin** but not prove deadly.

Some people assume that a falling coin will accelerate throughout its fall, at the mercy of gravity, until it hits the ground at high speed. However, repeated collisions with molecules in the air limit the coin's speed. This "drag force" increases with the coin's speed, eventually balancing the gravitational force, so the coin can no longer accelerate.

LIFE IN THE FAST LANE

The front and rear wings of a Formula 1 racing car create a huge downward force that stops the vehicle from overturning. The drag is so strong that, theoretically, it could counteract gravity, and these cars could be driven upside down when travelling faster than 160 kph (100 mph).

A coin dropped from the roof of the Empire State Building in New York, USA, would fall 381 m (1,250 ft) to the ground.

A coin's top speed, or terminal velocity, depends upon its shape and size, as well as the density of the air. For a 1 Euro coin, it is about 160 kph (100 mph).

coin increases the air resistance, thereby slowing the downward motion.

What are the top speeds of a falling skydiver, a tennis ball, and a raindrop?

MEDIEVAL WEAPONRY WAS POWERED BY GRAVITY

The trebuchet was a catapult used in the Middle Ages as a siege engine. It could fling projectiles weighing up to 160 kg (350 lb) at or into enemy fortifications. The machine was powered only by gravity, usually by means of a counterweight.

Gravity

Catapult

TREBUCHET

MOST ROLLERCOASTERS RELY ON GRAVITY

A chain pulls the cars up the first slope, providing them with gravitational potential energy, which is converted into kinetic energy as the cars roll down the slope, and then back into potential energy as they climb the next slope. As they trundle along the tracks, the cars continuously lose some of their kinetic energy due to friction and air resistance, so each successive "hill" is slightly less high than the last one – otherwise, they would not make it up the hill!

TRUE or FALSE? Toast lands butter-side down

What are the **chances**? If you drop toast, it's **odds-on** to hit the floor butter-side down. Splat! Similarly, a falling cat can thank its nine lives for landing safely on its feet **more often than not**. Though these are the **probable outcomes** of the two scenarios, there are reasons for both, and **no outcome is guaranteed**.

SHARED CELEBRATIONS

Sharing a birthday is often seen as a big coincidence, though it's anything but. In a group of only 23 people, there is a 50 per cent chance that two share the same birthday. The probability is very close to 100 per cent with 367 people, though it is 99 per cent with just 57 people.

If the average kitchen counter was twice as high, toast would land butter-side up 95 per cent of the time because there would be time for a complete rotation.

Toast lands butter-side down because of the height of a kitchen counter and the size of bread. There isn't enough time for toast to make a full rotation. The feline is built for freefall, with its highly flexible backbone enabling it to correct positions mid-air. Neither situation is a miracle – they are just more likely to happen than not.

The cat will usually flip over during the fall, letting its four feet absorb the shock on landing.

Cats have 30 spinal vertebrae compared to humans who have 24. This enables greater suppleness and versatility.

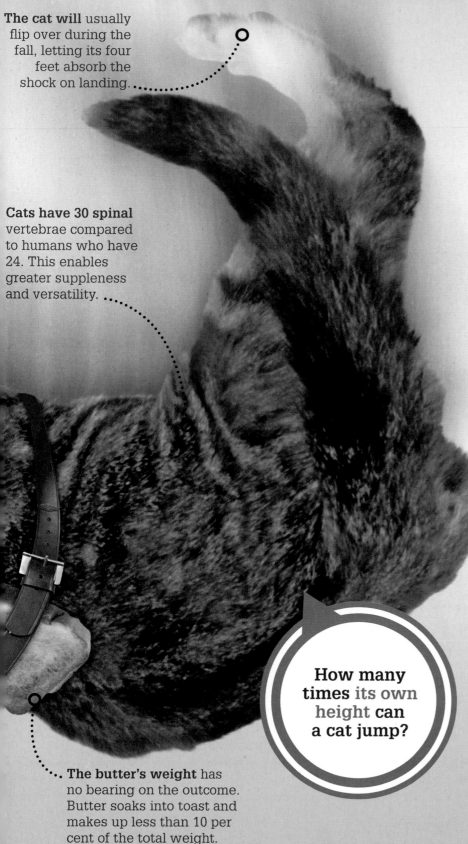

How many times its own height can a cat jump?

The butter's weight has no bearing on the outcome. Butter soaks into toast and makes up less than 10 per cent of the total weight.

FAST FACTS

DISEASES ARE THE MOST PROBABLE CAUSE OF DEATH

The chances of dying of heart disease are 1 in 5, with cancer close behind at 1 in 7. Only 6 per cent of deaths are due to accidents, but this adds up to more than three million deaths a year.

WALKING INTO A LAMPPOST
360 MILLION TO 1

LIGHTNING STRIKE
10 MILLION TO 1

FALLING DOWN A MANHOLE
5 MILLION TO 1

COMPUTER GAME EXHAUSTION
1.5 MILLION TO 1

THERE IS ALWAYS A 1 IN 2 CHANCE THAT A COIN WILL LAND HEADS UP

It's tempting to think that if you have tossed two heads in a row, the next toss is more likely to be a tail. In fact, it is equally likely to be another head.

PYTHAGORAS THOUGHT OF ODD NUMBERS AS MALE AND EVEN NUMBERS AS FEMALE

The Greek mathematician lived in the sixth century BCE, but his calculations and theories are still used today. He wasn't alone with the male and female numbers, either – the Chinese philosophy of yin and yang holds the same view.

FAST FACTS

THE USA USES MORE THAN 50 TIMES THE ELECTRICITY PER PERSON AS KENYA

Electricity consumption is uneven around the world, with developed countries using the most. However, global electricity demand is expected to rise by 70 per cent by 2035 partly because of the growth of emerging economies in Africa, Asia, and the Middle East.

KENYA

USA

AN ELECTRIC EEL CAN DISCHARGE ELECTRICITY AT 600 VOLTS

Eels store electric charge in specialized cells that work like batteries. These cells all discharge at the same time when the eel is under threat, or attacking prey.

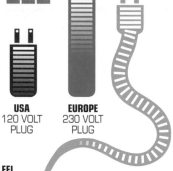

USA
120 VOLT
PLUG

EUROPE
230 VOLT
PLUG

EEL
600 VOLTS

The modern world relies upon electricity. Electric current is the flow of electric charge. In wires, it is electrically charged particles called electrons that move. They do this by huge electromagnetic machines called generators, which are typically powered by burning fossil fuels, such as oil or coal.

Leaving appliances off but plugged in is called vampire power because they still suck electricity from the wall socket.

Which bright spark invented the incandescent light bulb, fuses, switches, and sockets?

High-voltage electricity generated in power stations flows along cables attached to pylons. Devices called transformers, at electricity substations, reduce the voltage so it is safe to use in the home.

TRUE or FALSE? A screensaver saves electricity

At offices around the world, screensavers are **all in a day's work**. **Taking a break** from the computer **starts the screensaver**, but the electricity supply is not reduced. Far from a cost-cutting exercise, the computer is **still running a file**, making it **business as usual**.

A screensaver is usually activated for visual entertainment or computer security purposes.

GOING GREEN

Most electricity is generated in power stations burning coal, oil, or natural gas. But, increasingly, alternative sources, such as wind, water, and solar power are being used. In some countries, notably in South America, some electricity is generated using ethanol, a renewable fuel made from sugar cane (above).

TRUE or FALSE?

Glass is made of sand

This is not transparently obvious. It is strange to imagine grainy **sand** producing **smooth glass**, but sand is the main ingredient in the glass-making process. And it's nothing new. Ancient Egyptians made **glass beads** back in 3500 BCE.

Sand and other minerals are first shovelled into a blazing hot furnace. The intense heat fuses the mixture and melts it into liquid. The resulting molten liquid glass can be blown, moulded, poured, and pressed into different shapes, such as windows, ornaments, and lenses.

The addition of lead makes glass sparkle, while limestone strengthens glass, and iron oxide makes glass green.

Glass can be recycled indefinitely and not lose its quality.

SUPER-STRENGTH SYNTHETIC

Created in 1966, Kevlar is a flexible synthetic (manufactured) material. Five times stronger than steel but also very lightweight, it is ideal for protective clothing, such as bulletproof vests, as well as canoes, skis, and mobile phones.

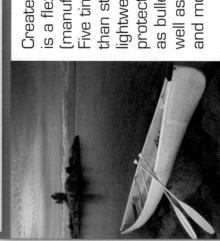

Who first produced transparent glass?

AFTER WATER, CONCRETE IS THE MOST WIDELY USED SUBSTANCE ON EARTH

5,000

The crucial ingredient in concrete is cement, which is made by mixing limestone with small amounts of clay and sand, and heating it in a kiln. Four billion tonnes of cement are produced each year. This is enough to make Egypt's Great Pyramid of Giza 5,000 times!

THE EIFFEL TOWER "GROWS" BY 15 CM (6 IN) IN SUMMER

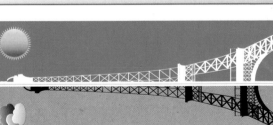

SUNLIGHT

SHADE

Steel expands when it is hot and contracts when it is cold. However, not all four sides of the structure can be in the Sun at once. The portion of the structure in direct sunlight expands more than the portion in the shade. This means that the tower can be leaning by up to 18 cm (7 in) at any one time.

TRUE or FALSE? Penicillin was found by accident

Accidents happen, and one took place in Scottish doctor Alexander Fleming's London laboratory on 28 September 1928. Mould that had landed accidentally on Fleming's Petri dish was producing a substance that **killed the bacteria** he was culturing. This was **penicillin**, the world's **first antibiotic**.

MICROWAVE MELTDOWN

When American engineer Percy Spencer (1894–1970) messed up with chocolate, it led to a modern-day marvel. As he inspected a magnetron (a device that produces microwave radiation for radar), the heat accidentally melted chocolate in his pocket. He developed the microwave oven as a result.

Blue-green mould had grown in the Petri dish because it was mistakenly left open.

While studying influenza, Fleming saw that a dish being used to grow the staphylococcus germs had accidentally developed mould. This had made a bacteria-free ring around itself. Australian scientist Howard Florey and German scientist Ernst Chain worked to produce penicillin as a pharmaceutical drug in the 1940s, and in 1945, Florey and Chain won the Nobel Prize for Medicine.

The discovery of penicillin led to the development of antibiotics – a range of medicines used to treat bacterial infections. Antibiotics have since saved millions of lives.

How did a mouldy melon get antibiotics into the mass market?

The mould was releasing a substance that stopped the bacteria's growth and instead developed a bacteria-free barrier around itself.

WE CAN THANK A DOG FOR VELCRO

Microscopic view of hooks and loops

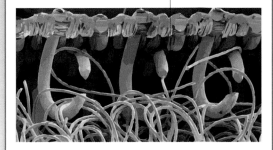

George de Mestral invented Velcro after taking his dog out for a walk. He noticed that the burrs (seeds) of burdock stuck to the dog's fur. Velcro works in the same way – tiny hooks on one strip of material cling to thin loops on another piece.

THE TIN OPENER WAS INVENTED

50 YEARS AFTER THE TIN CAN WAS FIRST PRODUCED

Early cans had to be opened using implements such as sharp knives, which was tricky because tins then were made with much thicker metal sheets than they are today. The tin opener made opening cans a lot less hazardous.

PLAY-DOH WAS INVENTED TO CLEAN WALLS

In the 1930s, coal was often used to heat homes, so Kutol Products invented a substance to remove soot stains from walls. But when schoolchildren began using the cleaner to make models in the 1950s, the product was repackaged and marketed as Play-Doh.

TRUE or FALSE? You can't be in two places at once

Time flies! Imagine making the most of it by being in **two places at once** – snoozing in bed, while still being on time for school. Unfortunately it's not possible for you, but modern science has shown **subatomic particles** can be in **millions of places** at once. At that teeny tiny size, life is in a **permanent state of flux**. Sigh! For now we can only dream.

EINSTEIN'S THEORIES

Modern physics is dominated by two amazing theories that reveal the world as very different from our everyday experience. Quantum theory deals with matter and energy at very small scales, while relativity deals with space and time. Both theories suggest the possibility of time travel and were pioneered by German physicist Albert Einstein (1879–1955) in the early 1900s.

Super small things can be in different places at once because they act both as particles and as waves. Light, for example, exists as waves, but also as a stream of particles called photons. Imagine a very dim light source that emits one photon at a time. Each photon exists as a wave spreading out in all directions – until it is detected in one place, as a tiny particle. This "wave-particle duality" is common to all subatomic particles, such as electrons and neutrinos – but not for larger objects like you.

Einstein worked out that if you travel faster than light, you would go back in time – but his theory of relativity showed that accelerating something beyond that speed is impossible.

According to the theory of relativity, time runs at different rates for different situations. There is no "absolute" rate of time – it is relative. The same is true of distances.

If you travel into Space at nearly the speed of light for a few years, and then return to Earth, you will find that much more time has passed back home than it has for you.

The most accurate clock on Earth is a type of atomic clock called strontium lattice. It won't lose a second in five billion years.

Where on Earth do clocks run the fastest?

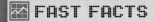

ANSWER TO EVERYTHING

QUANTUM COMPUTERS WILL HAVE THE

Extremely powerful quantum computers will be able to solve difficult problems very quickly. They will do so by considering all the possible answers simultaneously before coming up with one informed solution.

YOU CREATE A PARALLEL UNIVERSE EVERY TIME YOU MAKE A DECISION

That's according to one interpretation of quantum theory. For each important decision or action you take, there is another Universe in which you do something differently. The parallel versions of you also make decisions, which results in even more Universes. As we can't interact with parallel Universes, we may never know for sure whether or not they exist.

GRAVITY IS THE LAST PIECE IN THE COSMIC PUZZLE OF CREATION

According to quantum theory, forces are carried by subatomic particles. Scientists have discovered the particles that carry each of the forces – except gravity. If they exist, the particles that carry gravity, dubbed "gravitons", will be extremely hard to detect.

TRUE or FALSE? The Internet and the World Wide Web are the same thing

The Internet slows down when other continents wake up and log on.

SOCIAL NETWORKING

The 21st century has seen the rise of social networking. The number of people signed up to Facebook – a website used by friends to keep in touch – reached one billion in 2012. Another hugely popular site, Twitter, has more than 250 million members sharing short messages called "tweets".

Early computers filled up a room, but today's micro-technology has resulted in light, portable smartphones, tablets, and laptop computers. As computers have got smaller, so has the world. The Internet has given its users the opportunity to be in constant contact across the continents, with shared access to live news, realtime conversations, and a vast volume of on-line information.

Don't get your **wires crossed**! It's easy to get **techno-terms** muddled up, but make no mistake here. The Internet is a **network** of computers and cables, while the Web is the **collection of pages** surfed on-line.

Internet users around the world can choose to log on to any of tens of billions of websites.

Which continent has the most Internet users?

FAST FACTS

MORE THAN 75 PER CENT OF ALL EMAILS ARE CONSIDERED SPAM AND LEFT UNOPENED

The first commercial spam message was sent in 1978, but the definition of the word "spam" as unwanted messages was not added to a major English dictionary until 1998. About 183 billion spam messages are sent every day.

TWITTER USERS SEND OVER 340,000 NEW TWEETS EACH MINUTE

And YouTube users upload 100 hours of new video every minute. There are tens of billions of websites, and this number is growing all the time as new websites are created.

THE SPACE BAR

IS THE MOST POPULAR KEY ON A KEYBOARD

Taking keyboards and mobile phones together, at any given second the space bar is pressed six million times. This means that in the split-second you press the space bar, there are 600,000 others around the world doing the same thing. The next most popular key worldwide is the letter "e".

TRUE or FALSE? You are caught on CCTV 300 times a **day**

Can you really be **caught on camera** so many times? This number came from a book called *The Maximum Surveillance Society*, published in 1999. The true number of times **depends on location**. Off the beaten track, you may **never be seen**, but in the bright lights of the big city, you can't be **camera-shy**!

CCTV cameras are mainly used for crime prevention, travel problems, and crowd control.

It is estimated there are up to six million CCTV (Closed Circuit Television) cameras in use in the UK. Exact numbers are difficult to gauge as CCTV usage is constantly on the increase and many cameras are privately owned. Opposers complain that it creates a "Big Brother" state in which people have no privacy.

UP YOUR STREET

Google Street View and Google Earth are applications that map the world and the streets where people live. Special cars with street-view cameras on top travel around taking 360 degree views of neighbourhoods.

FAST FACTS

GOOGLE MAPS TECHNOLOGY HAS PINPOINTED DANGEROUS LAND MINES IN POST-WAR KOSOVO

This has allowed mines to be cleared safely. Google Maps is the most used smartphone application in the world. It combines satellite, aerial, and street level imagery.

SOME SATELLITES IN SPACE CAN SEE OBJECTS JUST 12 CM (5 IN) WIDE ON EARTH

12 CM (5 IN)

Observation satellites are like giant telescopes that are pointed at Earth. They gather information for weather forecasting, map-making, and environmental monitoring.

Does CCTV improve people's behaviour?

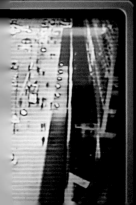

Robots will take over the world

The modern world has been **revolutionized by robots** – automated machines programmed to perform tasks. At least **10 million robots** exist, but world domination is beyond them. Robots cannot show initiative or react spontaneously. They are always ultimately **following human instruction**.

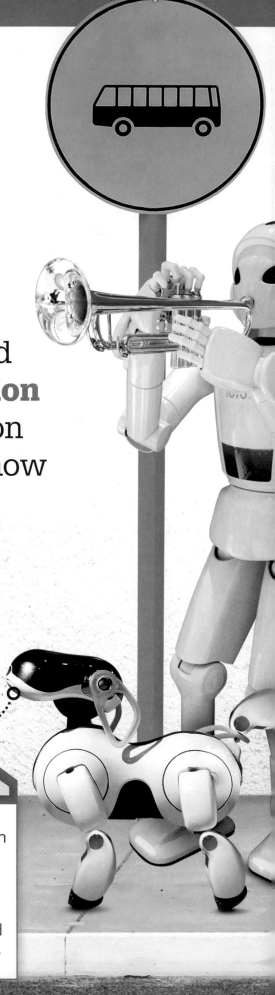

Sony's AIBO is a robot dog, designed to move and behave like a real canine.

CHESS CHAMPION

In 2006 Russian Vladimir Kramnik was chess champion of the world, but he was still to face his biggest opponent. In the Man Versus Machine competition held in Bonn, Germany, a computer named Deep Fritz beat Kramnik 4:2.

FAST FACTS

THE FIRST EVER ROBOT WAS A STEAM-POWERED BIRD

It was built from wood in ancient Greece by Archytas of Tarentum about 2,500 years ago. The bird managed to fly 200 m (656 ft) before running out of steam.

THERE ARE ABOUT 5,000 ROBOTS IN THE US MILITARY

These robots carry out dangerous work such as bomb disposal and landmine detection. This means that servicemen and women no longer have to risk their lives doing such tasks themselves.

Robots range from basic, mechanical toys for children through to complicated technologies, programmed with artificial intelligence, such as problem-solving and decision-making. They save employers time and money by working fast at repetitive tasks without the risks of fatigue or human error.

Toyota's robot is a humanoid robot, or android, but most robots don't need to resemble people to be useful.

Most surgical robots carry out procedures remotely on behalf of a surgeon who oversees the operation on screen and takes control of the robotic movements.

This builder robot is a concept idea. Most industry robots are computer-controlled mechanical arms on production lines.

How many car production workers are robots?

Honda's ASIMO can climb up and down stairs, and has a camera in its head to detect obstacles.

Cool science

SEEING THE **LIGHT**

Visible light, from red to violet, is part of the electromagnetic spectrum, which also includes other types of **electromagnetic radiation**. It runs from long-wavelength radio waves to short-wavelength gamma rays.

X-ray technology has revealed the **layers of paint** in Leonardo da Vinci's *Mona Lisa*. She once had **eyebrows** but they were painted out.

An incandescent light bulb turns only **three per cent** of electrical energy into light.

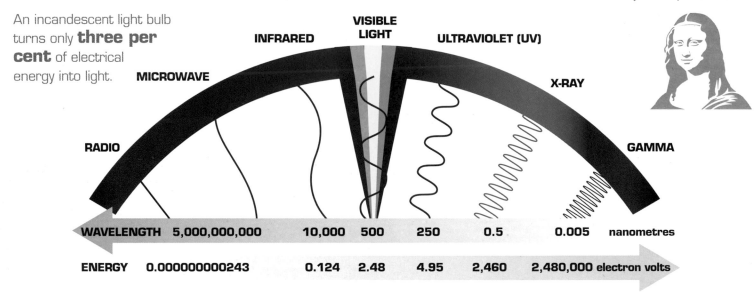

WAVELENGTH	5,000,000,000		10,000	500	250	0.5	0.005	nanometres
ENERGY	0.000000000243		0.124	2.48	4.95	2,460	2,480,000	electron volts

RADIO — MICROWAVE — INFRARED — VISIBLE LIGHT — ULTRAVIOLET (UV) — X-RAY — GAMMA

On a sunny day about **1,000 trillion** photons (light particles) hit an area the size of a pinhead each second.

LIFE **SAVERS** ➕

Vaccination prevents more than **TWO MILLION** deaths every year.

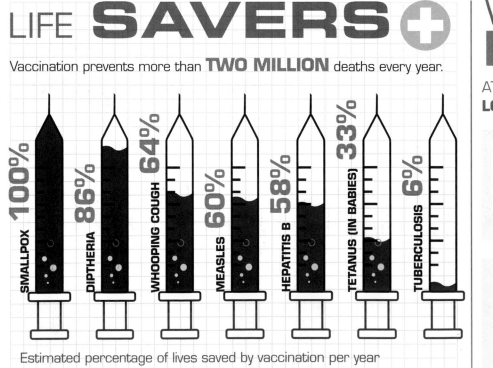

- SMALLPOX **100%**
- DIPTHERIA **86%**
- WHOOPING COUGH **64%**
- MEASLES **60%**
- HEPATITIS B **58%**
- TETANUS (IN BABIES) **33%**
- TUBERCULOSIS **6%**

Estimated percentage of lives saved by vaccination per year

WHAT'S THAT **NOISE?**

AT **115 DECIBELS**, A **BABY'S CRY** IS **LOUDER** THAN A TYPICAL **CAR HORN**

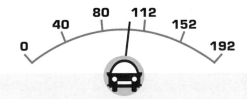

Decibel level at one metre's distance

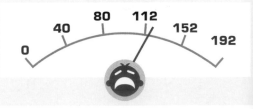

ON THE MOVE

A sheep, a duck, and a rooster became the first aircraft passengers when they flew in the Montgolfier Brothers' hot-air balloon in 1783.

The **Airbus A380** is the largest passenger aircraft, and can carry **853 people.** The smallest piloted aircraft ever made was the **Bumble Bee II**, which was large enough for only the person flying it.

Bumble Bee II wingspan: **1.68 m** (5.6 ft)

Airbus A380 wingspan: **79.8 m** (261.8 ft)

GREAT **INVENTIONS** OVER THE YEARS

LIGHTHOUSE
c 280 BCE

FIREWORKS
c 1000 CE o

TELESCOPE
1608 o

ELECTRONIC COMPUTER
1940s o

SMARTPHONE
2007 o

| 500 BCE | 0 | 500 CE | 1000 CE | 1500 CE | 2000 CE |

SCISSORS
c 100 CE o

PRINTING PRESS o
1455

TELEPHONE o
1876

WORLD WIDE WEB
1990 o

Space

Since the Big Bang started the Universe, the intergalactic discoveries and developments haven't stopped. But with so much still to explore, there have been some astronomical assumptions along the way and plenty of black holes left to unravel. Your Space odyssey starts here…

This stunning view of the Tarantula Nebula is taken by the Hubble Space Telescope. It shows millions of young stars bathed in ultraviolet, visible, and red light.

TRUE or FALSE? The Big Bang was loud

The Universe began in an **explosive split-second** about 13.7 billion years ago, but it didn't go off with a bang! Sound must have a material through which to **transmit its vibrations**, so before everything started, there was no way to **"hear"** it. Instead it was a silent spectacular we call the Big Bang.

Heat left over from the Big Bang is called cosmic microwave background radiation.

Until the Universe was three minutes old, its matter was nearly all hydrogen and helium atoms.

The Universe's first starry galaxies developed in the most densely packed areas.

BEIGE UNIVERSE

In 2002 American astronomers studied the average colour of the Universe and declared it to be… beige. From looking at all the light in Space and surveying more than 200,000 galaxies, they compared the creamy beige results to a milky coffee. The colour of the Universe is now "Cosmic Latte".

Starting off quiet, hot, and smaller than a full stop, the Universe has been getting noisier, cooler, and much, much bigger ever since. A trillionth of a second after the Big Bang, the Universe grew supersized in a period called the inflation era. It then slowed down to expand more steadily.

The temperature of the early Universe was a scorching 10 billion trillion trillion degrees Celsius.

What are the **Big Rip,** the **Big Crunch,** and the **Big Freeze?**

FAST FACTS

IN SPACE NO ONE CAN HEAR YOU SCREAM

Sound waves need a medium such as air or water to travel through. So, in the vacuum of Space, screams cannot be heard.

THE SUN
5,500°C (9,900°F)

EARTH
15°C (59°F)

NEPTUNE
-201°C (-330°F)

SPACE DOESN'T HAVE A TEMPERATURE

Space doesn't have a temperature, but the objects within the Universe do. Temperatures range from way below freezing to super hot.

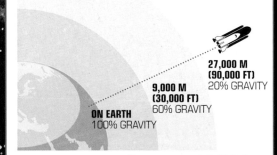

27,000 M
(90,000 FT)
20% GRAVITY

9,000 M
(30,000 FT)
60% GRAVITY

ON EARTH
100% GRAVITY

THERE IS GRAVITY IN SPACE

Small levels of gravity can be found everywhere in Space, but it weakens with distance. As a rocket travels further and further from Earth, it feels less and less of the planet's gravitational pull.

TRUE or FALSE? The Universe is getting bigger

In the first **three minutes of existence**, the Universe took off in a big way – from something billions of times smaller than a **tiny atom** to a **whopper** the size of our home galaxy, the Milky Way. It has been **expanding ever since**.

In the space beyond the Milky Way there are about 10 dwarf galaxies orbiting it.

MISSING UNIVERSE

Matter we know and recognize, such as planets and galaxies, makes up less than five per cent of the total Universe. Most of the Universe is unknown matter, named dark matter, and an unseen energy, named dark energy. Neither are visible, but their impact is clear on what we can see.

Earth, the Sun, and the stars at night are all part of the Milky Way. There are now about 400 billion stars in our galaxy. Though the first stars lived and died during the first billion years of the Universe, the remnants led to the birth of billions of new stars.

How many planets are there in the Milky Way Galaxy?

As well as stars, the galaxy contains dust and gas, held together by gravity...

FAST FACTS

THE UNIVERSE IS EXPANDING BY ABOUT 72 KM (45 MILES) EVERY SECOND

That's a whopping 6,000,000 km (3,700,000 miles) every hour! While you are asleep at night, it grows by 50 million km (30 million miles).

ELLIPTICAL   SPIRAL   IRREGULAR

THE **BIGGEST** GALAXIES LOOK LIKE SQUASHED BALLS

BARRED SPIRAL

Galaxies can be one of four shapes – elliptical (oval-shaped), spiral (disc-shaped with bright, curving lanes of stars), irregular (no defined shape), and barred spiral (spiral with a bar-shape in the middle).

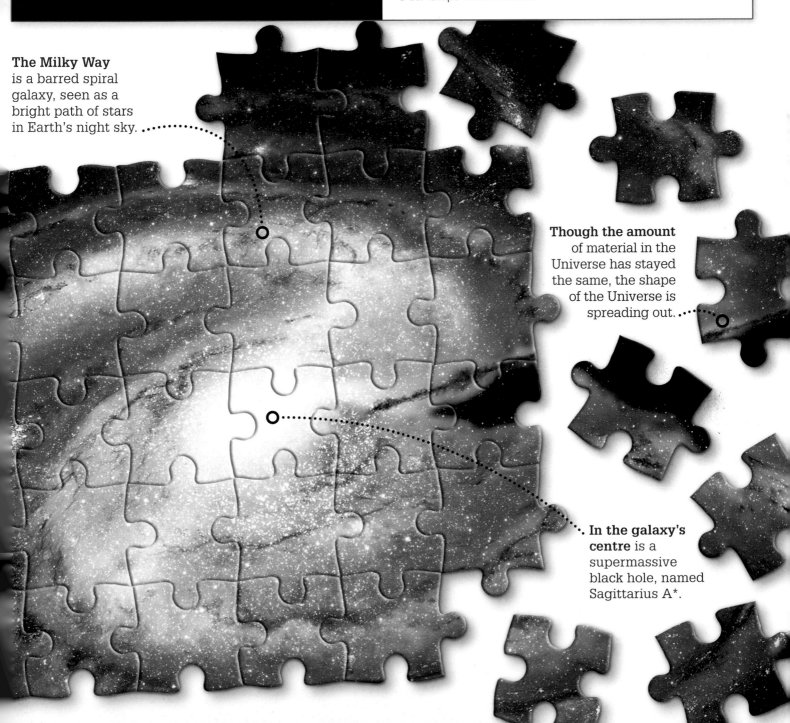

The Milky Way is a barred spiral galaxy, seen as a bright path of stars in Earth's night sky.

Though the amount of material in the Universe has stayed the same, the shape of the Universe is spreading out.

In the galaxy's centre is a supermassive black hole, named Sagittarius A*.

TRUE or FALSE? A black hole sucks in everything near it

This is not the whole story. The **gravitational pull** of a black hole is undeniably strong, but it **cannot absorb** all matter. Mysterious **dark matter** seems able to resist it.

The opening of the hole is called the "event horizon". If an object crosses this point, it can never escape.

SUPERMASSIVE HOLES

A basic black hole is just one collapsed star, but the centre of a galaxy is home to a supermassive black hole. This is millions of times heavier and more massive, with far stronger gravitational force.

A **stellar black hole** forms when a massive star dies, but we don't know exactly how supermassive black holes are formed. These holes are black because no light can escape from inside. The first black hole to be discovered was Cygnus X-1 during the 1970s.

The ergosphere is the area around the event horizon. An object in the ergosphere can still exit the black hole.

What might happen if you fell into a black hole?

YOU CAN'T SEE A BLACK HOLE

The powerful gravity pulls light into the middle of the black hole, so it's invisible. Scientists know black holes exist from watching how the gravity affects the stars and gas around them.

TIME STOPS IN

00:00

A BLACK HOLE

The black hole's gravity distorts time, which runs slower near the hole. Time appears to stop once an object has crossed the event horizon, and seems to become frozen inside Space.

THE BLACK HOLE IN THE MILKY WAY HAS THE MASS OF

4 MILLION SUNS

The smallest black holes may be a single atom but with the mass of a large mountain. This shows how dense they are — so dense that nothing can escape their amazing gravitational pull.

Only Saturn has rings

Saturn is the Solar System's **ring leader**, but all the other **gas giants** have rings, too. The rings of Jupiter, Neptune, and Uranus **contain less material**, so they are harder to spot.

Jumbo Jupiter is the fastest spinning planet, whirling round at more than double the speed of Earth.

Great Red Spot

SPOTTY STORMS

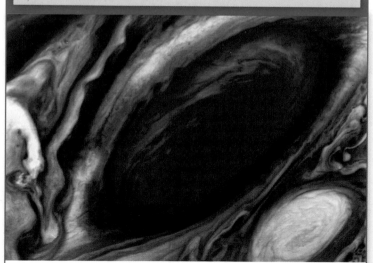

The biggest storm in the Solar System is raging on Jupiter. Called the Great Red Spot, it is twice the size of Earth and has been there for at least 300 years. The combination of Jupiter's speedy spin and wild winds produce mega-storms, creating spots on the surface.

Jupiter has more than 60 moons, including Ganymede, the biggest moon in the Solar System.

It is often assumed that Saturn has a solitary ring, but up close there are hundreds of them. Each one consists of millions of bits of dirty ice. From tiny dust particles to huge rocks, these pieces whizz their way around the planet. The rings of the other three giants are made the same way, though much less visible.

URANUS IS THE ONLY PLANET TO SPIN ON ITS SIDE

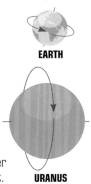

EARTH

URANUS

It's possible that an object the size of Earth crashed into Uranus in the past and knocked it over. All the other planets spin almost upright.

ALL THE PLANETS COULD FIT INSIDE JUPITER

MARS JUPITER VENUS

EARTH MERCURY

URANUS NEPTUNE

SATURN

In fact, Jupiter is such a whopper you could put the other planets inside it, and there would still be room to spare.

JUPITER
11.86 YEARS

SUN

NEPTUNE
164.9 YEARS

EARTH
1 YEAR

IT TAKES NEPTUNE 164.9 EARTH YEARS TO ORBIT THE SUN

This is the longest planetary orbit of the Sun. It takes Uranus about 84 Earth years, Saturn about 29.5 Earth years, and Jupiter about 12 Earth years.

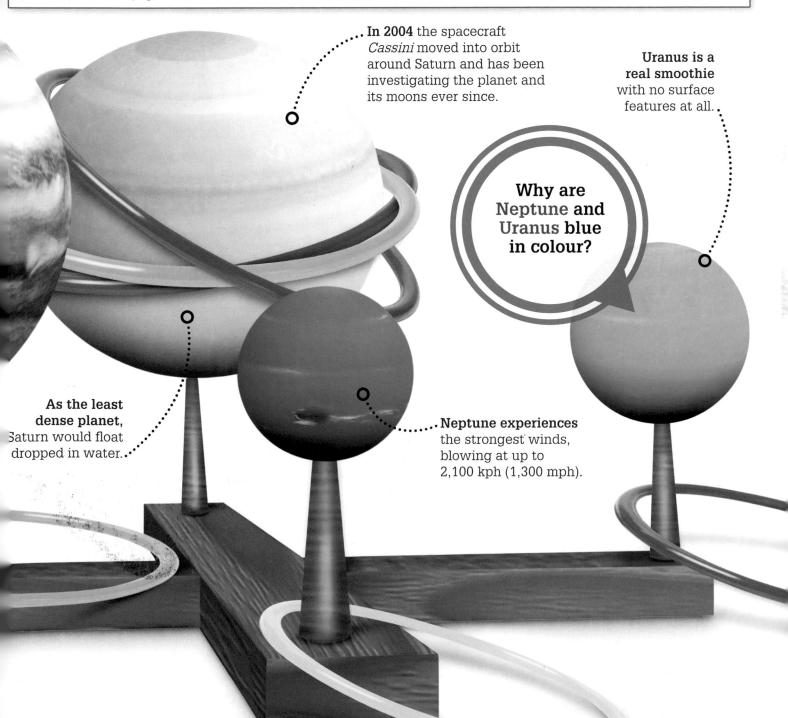

In 2004 the spacecraft *Cassini* moved into orbit around Saturn and has been investigating the planet and its moons ever since.

Uranus is a real smoothie with no surface features at all.

Why are Neptune and Uranus blue in colour?

As the least dense planet, Saturn would float dropped in water.

Neptune experiences the strongest winds, blowing at up to 2,100 kph (1,300 mph).

TRUE or FALSE? There has **never** **been** life on Mars

Earth is the only place in the Universe where life is known to exist, but fellow **rocky world Mars** may also have produced life. This **red planet** was once **warm and wet**. Where water flows, there is the **possibility of life**, though maybe not as we know it...

LONG-HAUL VOYAGERS

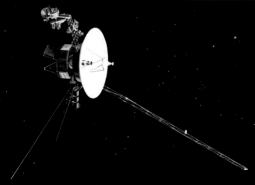

Even if we can't find life on Mars, it may exist elsewhere. Twin Voyager spacecraft are on a mission to attract alien interest. On board is the golden record, detailing the history of humans. Launched by NASA in 1977, they'll arrive at the next planetary system in 80,000 years. So, watch this Space...

Mars is now cold and dry with empty river beds and cracked floodplains, but the lakes and seas that formed in its craters three billion years ago would have been suitable environments for early life forms to thrive. Only 100 years ago, some observers believed the network of barren canals on Mars was the result of hardworking aliens!

Wind blows dust into the air, making the sky red.

Giant volcanoes and deep canyons are surface features.

Robot rover *Curiosity* has been exploring Mars since 2012, looking for signs that it was once home to tiny life forms.

The extendable arm of *Curiosity* stretches 2 m (7 ft) to study a rock at close range.

How fast does *Curiosity* travel across the surface of Mars?

Dusty red soil covers the surface of Mars.

FAST FACTS

MERCURY BLOWS HOT AND COLD

SUN

Nighttime -180°C (-290°F)

Daytime 430°C (800°F)

MERCURY

The temperature on this rocky planet ranges from a fiery 430°C (800°F) in the day to a bitterly cold -180°C (-290°F) at night.

Carbon dioxide atmosphere

Sulphuric acid

Rocky mantle

Metallic core

VENUS

VENUS IS NAMED AFTER THE ROMAN GODDESS OF LOVE AND BEAUTY

This is an unlikely pairing, since Venus is a hot, hostile rocky planet, surrounded by clouds of corrosive sulphuric acid.

MARS IS HALF THE SIZE OF EARTH

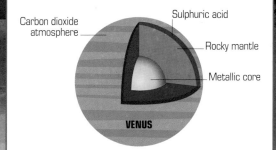

6,800 km (4,220 miles) diameter

12,756 km (7,926 miles) diameter

MARS

EARTH

But Mars has no oceans and is land all over, so its land covers about the same area as that of our home planet.

TRUE or FALSE?
Pluto is a planet

Discovered in 1930, Pluto became the ninth honorary member of the **planetary party**. The party was over in 2006 when astronomers **reclassified it a dwarf planet**. Now Pluto keeps company with the other dwarf planets, and **more are likely** to join them.

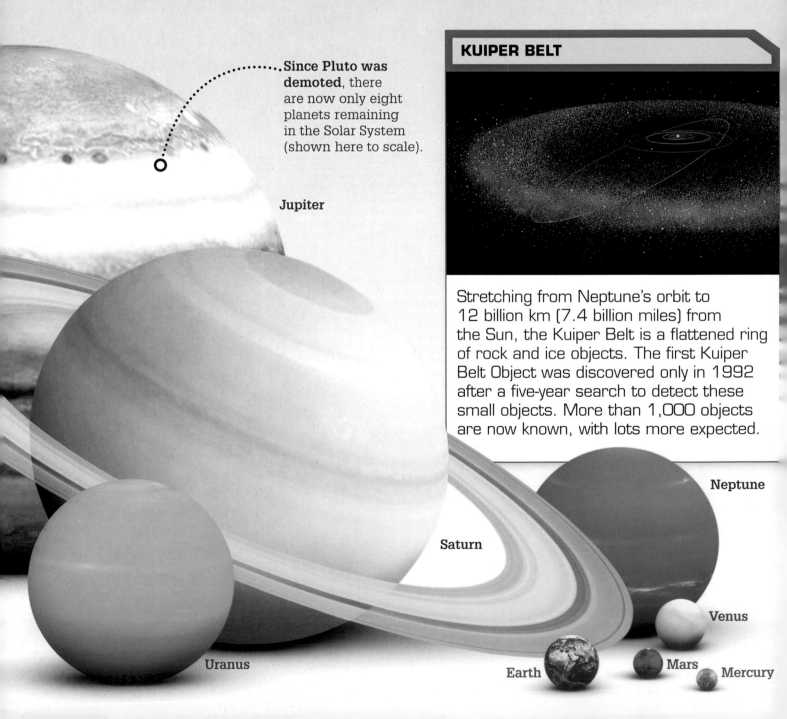

Since Pluto was demoted, there are now only eight planets remaining in the Solar System (shown here to scale).

Jupiter

KUIPER BELT

Stretching from Neptune's orbit to 12 billion km (7.4 billion miles) from the Sun, the Kuiper Belt is a flattened ring of rock and ice objects. The first Kuiper Belt Object was discovered only in 1992 after a five-year search to detect these small objects. More than 1,000 objects are now known, with lots more expected.

Neptune

Saturn

Venus

Uranus

Earth

Mars

Mercury

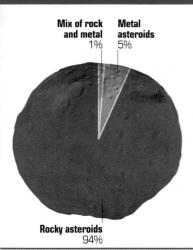

Mix of rock
and metal
1%

Metal
asteroids
5%

Rocky asteroids
94%

ASTEROIDS
ARE MADE OF
ALL SORTS

Billions of asteroids orbit the Sun. Most are rocky, while the rest are made of metal, or a mix of rock and metal. Metallic asteroids are mostly made of iron, but may also include platinum and even gold.

2006
Left Earth

2007
Passed
Jupiter

New Horizons
probe

2015
Reaches
Pluto

IT TAKES NEARLY A DECADE
TO REACH PLUTO

Launched by NASA in 2006 and due to arrive in 2015, the *New Horizons* spacecraft is on a mission to explore Pluto and its moons. Having passed Jupiter and taken a photograph of a volcano on Jupiter's moon Io, this plucky craft will have travelled nearly 5 billion km (3 billion miles) to reach the dwarf planet.

In 2006 astronomers introduced the class of dwarf planets. This new group consists of rocky balls much smaller than the main planets of the Solar System but still planet-like in shape. They include Pluto, Eris, Haumea, and Makemake. All four orbit the Sun as part of a gang of icy rock bodies and whizzing comets that live in the Space neighbourhood beyond the planets.

Pluto is smaller than Earth's Moon. The surface temperature here is -230°C (-380°F), even in summer!

Covered in a thick coating of ice, Pluto has a rocky interior.

Makemake takes 310 years to go around the Sun – the longest time of all the dwarf planets.

What is the story behind Pluto's name?

◀ **PLANETS**

NON-PLANETS ▶

Haumea is egg-shaped.

Eris is the largest dwarf planet.

Earth is the largest rocky planet. Its crust consists of seven large moving plates that rub together, making mountains and volcanoes. The landscape is constantly changing from the effects of wind, water, ice, and ranging temperatures, as well as the impact of human activity and settlement.

What are the record temperature highs and lows on Earth?

The Equator receives the most sunlight, while the North and South poles get the least.

During the last 10,000 years, 25 per cent of Earth's forests have been cleared to create farm land and build houses.

WATCHING THE WORLD

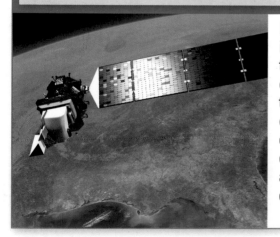

Launched in 2013, *Landsat 8* is now orbiting our planet. It is the latest in a series of Landsat craft that together have made the longest continuous record of Earth's land from Space. Other craft collect data on our planet's oceans and atmosphere, as well as topical issues such as climate change and car emissions.

More than two-thirds of Earth's surface is water.

TRUE or FALSE? Earth is a perfect sphere

Astronauts dubbed our planet the **"blue marble"**, but the notion that it is spherical goes pear-shaped. With its mountains and valleys, it is clear that **Earth's lumps and bumps** can never be whipped into perfect shape. Instead our planet is an **oblate spheroid** – a sphere squashed at the ends and swollen in the middle.

Earth's circumference is 40,074 km (24,900 miles).

Earth's oceans formed when steam in the young planet's atmosphere condensed into water and fell to the surface.

FAST FACTS

EARTH IS THE DENSEST OF ALL THE PLANETS

This is because Earth contains a lot of iron. Both its solid inner core and molten outer core are mainly iron, while the rest of the core is nickel.

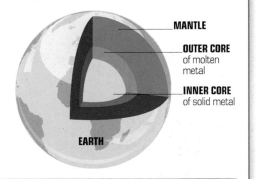

MANTLE

OUTER CORE
of molten metal

INNER CORE
of solid metal

EARTH

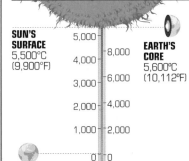

SUN'S SURFACE 5,500°C (9,900°F)	5,000 / 8,000
	4,000
EARTH'S CORE 5,600°C (10,112°F)	
	3,000 / 6,000
	2,000 / 4,000
	1,000 / 2,000
EARTH AVERAGE GLOBAL TEMP 15°C (59°F)	0 / 0
	°C / °F

THE TEMPERATURE AT EARTH'S CORE IS 5,600°C (10,112°F)

That's as hot as the Sun's surface! Thankfully, Earth's surface is much cooler – the average global temperature is 15°C (59°F). The hottest regions of the surface are near the Equator, while the coldest are near its two poles.

TRUE or FALSE? There is a dark side of the Moon

Many moons ago, sky-gazers speculated about a **mysterious dark side** to the Moon that we never get to see because the **same near side** of the Moon **always faces Earth**. Thanks to **lunar landings and satellite surveillance**, we're no longer in the dark about the far side.

Photographs of the far side of the Moon have been taken, showing that the far side gets just as much sunlight as the near side.

TIDAL FORCE

The Moon produces the daily tides in Earth's oceans. Gravitational forces on the Moon pull on the water, creating bulges in the sea on either side of the planet. These bulges cause the regular rise and fall of the water level at the sea's edge that we call tides. The world's most extreme tides occur at the Bay of Fundy in Canada (shown at high and low tide).

Hundreds of millions of years ago, the Moon rotated much more quickly than it does today, taking less time to orbit Earth. As the Moon's gravity slowed Earth's spin, the Moon took longer to orbit Earth and its spin slowed down. Today the Moon takes 27.3 days to make one rotation on its axis, and to complete one orbit around our planet. As the rotation and orbit times are equal, the same side of the Moon is permanently visible to us on Earth.

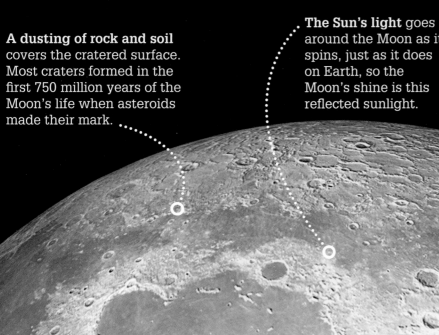

A dusting of rock and soil covers the cratered surface. Most craters formed in the first 750 million years of the Moon's life when asteroids made their mark.

The Sun's light goes around the Moon as it spins, just as it does on Earth, so the Moon's shine is this reflected sunlight.

Why does the Moon turn red during an eclipse?

FAST FACTS

IF YOU STEPPED ON THE MOON, YOUR FOOTPRINTS MIGHT STAY THERE FOREVER

This is because, unlike on Earth, there is no wind or water to blow or wash the footprints away. The Moon doesn't have volcanoes, either, so its surface stays the same. It is possible that future visitors may wipe out the footprints, or they could wear away as meteorites strike the surface of the Moon.

THE MOON IS THE MOST POPULAR DESTINATION FOR SPACECRAFT

Since the first one arrived in 1959, more than 60 spacecraft have visited the Moon. Astronauts on the *Apollo 8* spacecraft were the first to see the dark side of the Moon in 1968.

1959 *LUNA 3*
a flyby, took the first images of the far side

1969 *APOLLO 11*
first humans to land on the Moon

2007 *CHANG'E 1*
China's first lunar orbiter

2009 *LUNAR RECONNAISSANCE ORBITER*
currently mapping the Moon

THE US FLAG IS STILL ON THE MOON

A flag was planted there by US astronaut Neil Armstrong in 1969 when he became the first person to step on the Moon, but it was blown down by the rocket exhaust as the astronauts blasted off for home. However, flags from other Apollo missions still stand on the lunar surface.

TRUE or FALSE? The Sun is yellow

Children's drawings of **bright yellow sunshine** capture its true colour. This big ball of glowing gas is a **yellow star**. But there's nothing mellow about this yellow. The Sun is seriously **hot stuff**, with a **sizzling surface** of 5,500°C (9,900°F).

Where on Earth is it sunny during the night?

SOLAR POWER

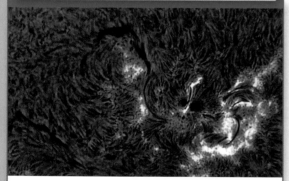

At close range, the Sun's surface is a hotbed of activity. Gas jets, called spicules, fire up repeatedly. Great looping clouds and swathes of cooler gas, called prominences, reach into Space. The distinctive orange peel texture of the surface, known as granulation, comes from gas cells rising up constantly.

Clouds, called prominences, extend into Space for hundreds of thousands of kilometres.

The Sun's rays take more than eight minutes to reach our skin.

The Sun looks yellow from Earth or Space, but it is more yellow from Earth due to the atmosphere. If you viewed the Sun from a mountain top, the yellow intensity would reduce because there is less air. We are so familiar with depictions of the yellow Sun that astronomers artificially enhance images to make them more yellow.

Spacecraft SOHO (Solar and Heliospheric Observatory) photographs the Sun and studies the surface.

White areas, called faculae, are the hottest regions of the Sun.

Darker sunspots are cooler areas of the Sun.

The circumference of the Sun is 4.4 million km (2.7 million miles).

The Sun is three-quarters hydrogen and almost all the rest is helium, held together by gravity.

FAST FACTS

THE SUN MAKES UP 99.8% OF THE OVERALL MASS OF THE SOLAR SYSTEM

0.2% Rest of the Solar System

99.8% Sun's mass

Everything in our Solar System revolves around this brilliant star. Up until the 16th century, however, it was believed that Earth was at the heart of everything, and the Sun and planets circled around it.

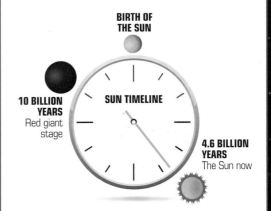

BIRTH OF THE SUN

10 BILLION YEARS
Red giant stage

SUN TIMELINE

4.6 BILLION YEARS
The Sun now

THERE WILL BE ANOTHER FIVE BILLION YEARS OF SUNSHINE

The Sun is currently middle-aged because its rays have already been shining for at least 4.6 billion years. Towards the end of its life, during the red giant stage, the Sun will expand to about 100 times its size, cool, and turn red. The Sun will start to die as material is shed from its outer layers. What remains of the dying star packs together to make a star about the same size as Earth, called a white dwarf. This fades and cools to become a cold, dark cinder in Space.

TRUE or FALSE? Starlight is millions of years old

When you look up at the stars, you're seeing their **original light** created many thousands or even millions of years before. A light year (ly) is the distance light travels in a year – a **mind-boggling** 9.46 millon million km (5.88 million million miles), so the light of a star **millions of ly** away has taken **millions of years** to reach us.

The atmosphere surrounding Earth makes stars appear to twinkle in the sky.

The light we see from these stars left before the Great Pyramid was built in Egypt.

JEWEL BOX Cluster of stars about 10 million years old

TARANTULA NEBULA Very young stars, between one and two million years old

STAR CYCLE

A star is born in a cloud of gas and dust. When nuclear reactions start, the star releases energy and shines steadily. It swells into a red giant or a supergiant. Most stars die slowly, but the massive ones explode as brilliant supernovas.

Stars produce different amounts of light. We find out which stars produce the most light by comparing their luminosity – the energy a star emits in just one second. The brightest stars release light more than six million times that of the Sun, while the least luminous stars create light less than one ten-thousandth.

Are there more stars in the sky or grains of sand on Earth?

Heat and light are produced when hydrogen turns into helium gas inside the star's core.

Massive stars can blow up, but we may not know for thousands of years. We see how the star looked when the light left years ago.

Light from these stars takes 16,000 years to reach Earth. This cluster is like a beehive swarm of 10 million stars.

THE HOTTEST STARS ARE **BLUE**

You might expect the hottest stars to be red, and the coolest to be blue, but in fact, it's the other way round. Blue stars reach a temperature of about 40,000°C (72,000°F), while red stars get no hotter than 4,000°C (7,200°F).

HOW A STAR DIES DEPENDS ON ITS MASS – THE AMOUNT OF MATERIAL IT IS MADE FROM

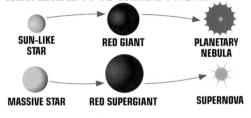

SUN-LIKE STAR → RED GIANT → PLANETARY NEBULA

MASSIVE STAR → RED SUPERGIANT → SUPERNOVA

Sun-like stars shine brightly for billions of years. Late in life they expand to become a cooler, brighter star called a red giant. It sheds its outer layers, called a planetary nebula. Stars with more than eight times the Sun's mass last only a few million years. They become supergiants, which explode as supernovas and leave a neutron star or a black hole behind.

OMEGA CENTAURI
Ancient stars more than 10 billion years old

FAST FACTS

EACH STAR IS CONSTANTLY MOVING IN SPACE

THE GREAT BEAR
50,000 years ago

THE GREAT BEAR
Today

Stars are constantly moving in Earth's sky, but it takes tens of thousands of years before new positions are noticeable, and constellations have new shapes. Yet it is possible to see changes since the ancient Greeks first identified constellations more than 2,500 years ago.

ALL THE BRIGHTEST STARS IN THE NIGHT SKY ARE LABELLED ALPHA

Stars are named within a constellation in order of brightness using the Greek alphabet, so the brightest stars begin "alpha", the next brightest "beta", and so on. Many of the stars we can see also have historical names, such as Betelgeuse, named by Arabic astronomers.

SIRIUS
Alpha CMa

BETELGEUSE
Alpha Ori

POLLUX
Beta Gem

ADHARA
Epsilon CMa

YOU CAN SEE MORE STARS OUT OF TOWN

On a clear, moonless night using just your eyes, about 300 stars are visible from the city, and about 1,000 in a darker village sky. In the darkest countryside about 3,000 are visible; use binoculars and you'll see more than 40,000.

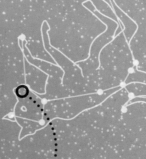

Why do some stars shine brighter in the night sky?

Part of Canis Major, Sirius (or "Dog Star") is the brightest star in the sky, burning 20 times brighter than the Sun.

Named after a mythical hunter in ancient Greece, Orion holds a club and a lion's head. He is followed by his canine companion, Canis Major.

Betelgeuse in the Orion constellation is one of the top ten brightest stars in the night sky.

Seen in Earth's southern hemisphere, Scorpius has a sting in its tail, killing Orion in Greek mythology.

One of the 12 zodiac constellations, Leo is a cave-dwelling lion described in Greek myths.

TRUE or FALSE?

Stars in a constellation are close together

The constellations may appear to contain connected stars, but they are vastly different distances from Earth. A different vantage point would rearrange the stars in a new pattern. However, the constellations are useful to stargazers tracking the night sky. Most of the constellations have been given two names – a Latin name and a common name. More than half are characters from ancient Greek mythology.

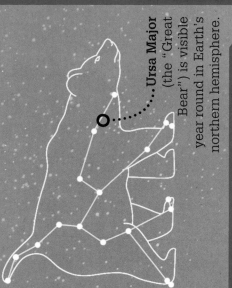

Ursa Major (the "Great Bear") is visible year round in Earth's northern hemisphere.

Though stars appear to shine in glittering groups, it is an **optical illusion**. Astronomers have divided the sky above Earth into **88 imaginary pieces**. Each is a constellation forming its own pattern, but the stars within it are really **spaced out**.

GALAXY GREATS

Swirling through our skies are galaxies containing masses of stars, dust, and dark matter. Each galaxy has a unique catalogue number to identify it. Some galaxies have novelty names to describe their shape, such as the cigar (shown), fried egg, sunflower, and sombrero.

Observatories house telescopes used to look deep into Space. The telescopes collect light that forms amazing magnified images of the stars and galaxies.

TRUE or FALSE? Astronauts would explode without Space suits

This double-layered bodysuit is known as a liquid cooling and ventilation garment (LCVG).

There would be no explosions, but it would still be the **final frontier**. Without Space suits, astronauts would die, either from the **freezing cold** or from their **blood boiling** due to the drop in pressure.

SPACE LIFE

The International Space Station (ISS) is about 390 km (240 miles) above Earth. Astronauts spend months here, working in the laboratories or carrying out station maintenance. There is a galley kitchen, exercise equipment, and sleep cabins. Sleeping bags are fixed so they cannot float away in the weightless conditions.

Gloves are thick enough to protect the hands but thin enough to allow ease of movement.

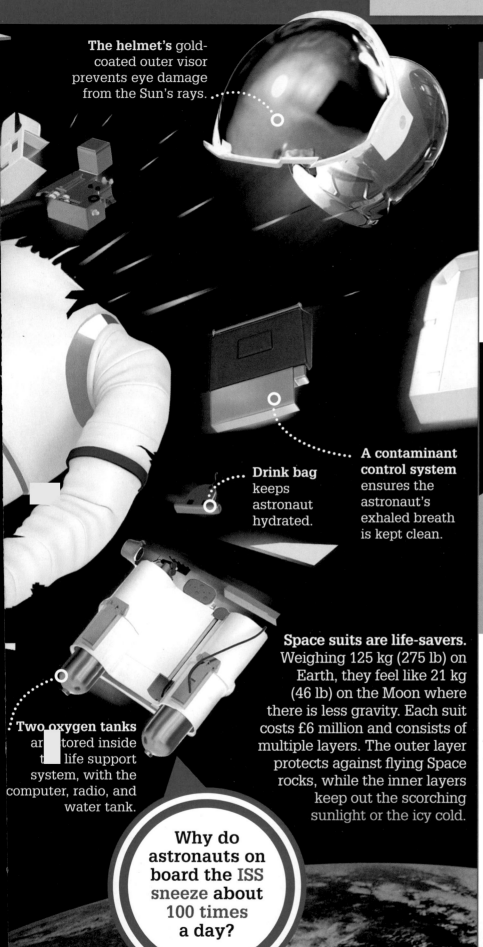

The helmet's gold-coated outer visor prevents eye damage from the Sun's rays.

Drink bag keeps astronaut hydrated.

A contaminant control system ensures the astronaut's exhaled breath is kept clean.

Two oxygen tanks are stored inside the life support system, with the computer, radio, and water tank.

Space suits are life-savers. Weighing 125 kg (275 lb) on Earth, they feel like 21 kg (46 lb) on the Moon where there is less gravity. Each suit costs £6 million and consists of multiple layers. The outer layer protects against flying Space rocks, while the inner layers keep out the scorching sunlight or the icy cold.

Why do astronauts on board the ISS sneeze about 100 times a day?

FAST FACTS

THE FIRST CHIMP TO GO INTO SPACE WAS CALLED HAM

This unusual Space traveller went aboard a US Mercury spacecraft in 1961. Other creatures to have reached Space include mice, monkeys, rabbits, guinea pigs, insects, cats, dogs, turtles, spiders, and even jellyfish.

A MODERN CAR IS MORE COMPLEX THAN APOLLO 11

In the early days, NASA sent astronauts to the Moon using less computing power than is found in a modern car. Still, the spacecraft was equipped with real-time flight information and an automatic navigation system, and it worked!

PIZZA HUT DO SPACE TAKEAWAYS

In 2001 Pizza Hut "delivered" a vacuum-sealed pizza to hungry astronauts on board the International Space Station. Admittedly, the Russian rocket carrying the takeaway took longer than the usual 30 minutes to arrive.

Out of this world

A UNIVERSAL VIEW

75% HYDROGEN

23% HELIUM

2% OTHER ELEMENTS

The elements **hydrogen** and **helium** make up **98 per cent** of the matter we can see in the **Universe**.

The most distant object that many people can see using just their eyes is the Andromeda Galaxy, **25 million million km** (15 million million miles) away.

MOON-GAZING

As the **Moon orbits Earth**, a changing amount of the one face we see is bathed by sunlight. The different shapes are the Moon's **phases**. One cycle of phases lasts **29.5 days**.

NEW MOON

WAXING CRESCENT

FIRST QUARTER

WAXING GIBBOUS

FULL MOON

WANING GIBBOUS

LAST QUARTER

WANING CRESCENT

NEW MOON

The maiden name of **moonwalking** astronaut Buzz Aldrin's mother was **Moon**.

SOLAR SYSTEM

Venus is the hottest planet in our Solar System. The surface is hot enough to **melt lead**.

464°C (867°F) — Venus

167°C (333°F) — Mercury

15°C (59°F) — Earth

-63°C (-81°F) — Mars

-108°C (-162°F) — Jupiter

-139°C (-218°F) — Saturn

-197°C (-323°F) — Uranus

-201°C (-330°F) — Neptune

500°
400°
100
0°
-100
-200

The Solar System's **largest volcano** is **Olympus Mons** on Mars. It is **610 km (380 miles)** wide. That's about the **same width as Spain**.

SEEING STARS

If you counted all the stars in the **Milky Way** at the rate of **one a second,** it would take you about **12,000 years** to count them all.

The **biggest** diamond is in the heart of an old star named **BPM 37093** with a diameter of **4,000 km** (2,485 miles). That's roughly the width of Australia.

LIFT OFF!

Many countries have spaceflight **launch sites.** Sites closer to the Equator can launch heavier cargo, because rockets there are given a boost by **the speed of Earth's spin**.

Baikonur, Kazakhstan

Cape Canaveral, USA

Xjchang, China

Kourou, French Guiana

FIVE ASTRONAUT FIRSTS

1961 — **Yuri Gagarin** first human in Space (Russian)

1963 — **Valentina Tereshkova** first woman in Space (Russian)

1965 — **Alexei Leonov** first to spacewalk (Russian)

1969 — **Neil Armstrong** first to walk on the Moon (American)

2001 — **Dennis Tito** first Space tourist (American)

Each **toilet** on the **International Space Station** cost £11 million ($19 million).

MAKING AN IMPACT

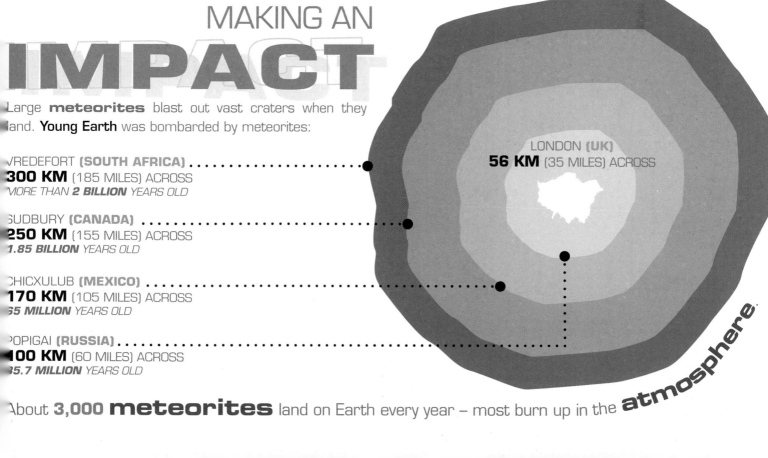

Large **meteorites** blast out vast craters when they land. **Young Earth** was bombarded by meteorites:

VREDEFORT (SOUTH AFRICA) ....
300 KM (185 MILES) ACROSS
*MORE THAN **2 BILLION** YEARS OLD*

SUDBURY (CANADA) ....
250 KM (155 MILES) ACROSS
1.85 BILLION YEARS OLD

CHICXULUB (MEXICO) ....
170 KM (105 MILES) ACROSS
65 MILLION YEARS OLD

POPIGAI (RUSSIA) ....
100 KM (60 MILES) ACROSS
35.7 MILLION YEARS OLD

LONDON (UK)
56 KM (35 MILES) ACROSS

About **3,000 meteorites** land on Earth every year – most burn up in the *atmosphere*.

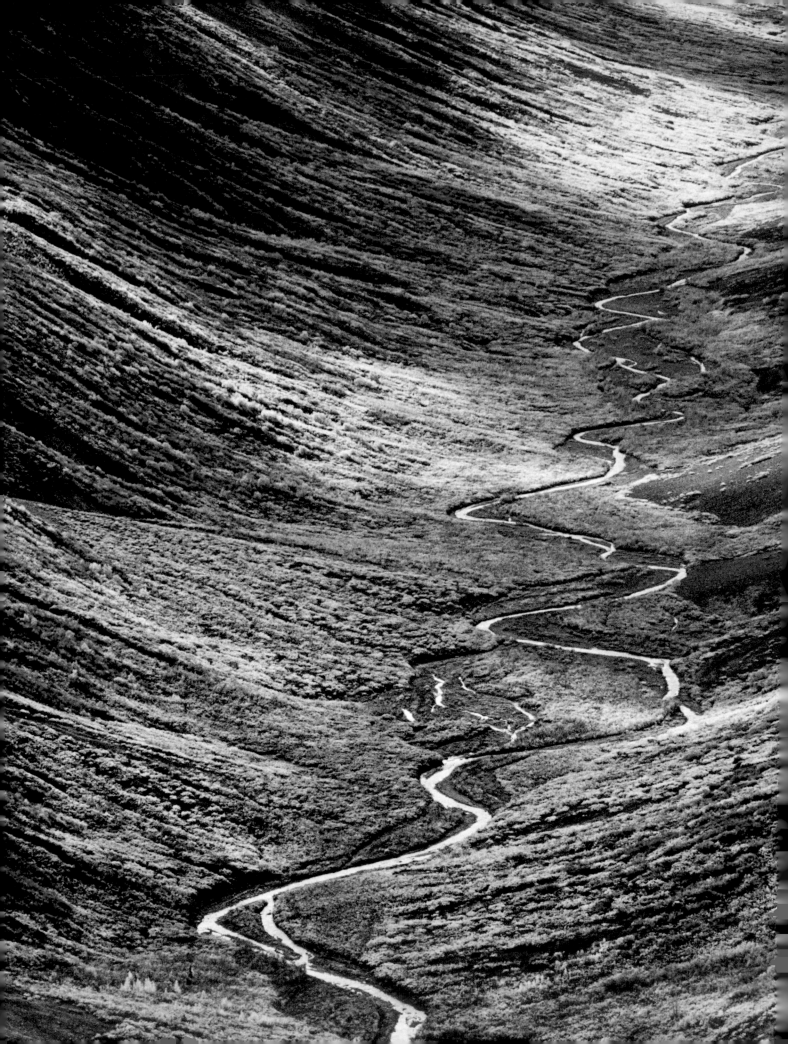

Earth

Our planet has been shaped over millions of years by tectonic forces, climate change, and weather. Some features develop slowly, such as mountains, while others occur rapidly, such as earthquakes. The truth about these processes and influences is often worlds apart from the myriad misconceptions about Earth.

This aerial view shows a river meandering through a U-shaped valley in Wrangell-St. Elias National Park, USA. Originally V-shaped, the valley was altered by ice erosion.

TRUE or FALSE? India was once joined to Australia

Earth's surface consists of **tectonic plates**, which fit together like a **jigsaw puzzle**. The continents we recognize today sit on six of these plates and were formed when large **supercontinents** broke up and **drifted apart**. The supercontinent **Gondwana** connected India and Australia, along with Africa, South America, and Antarctica.

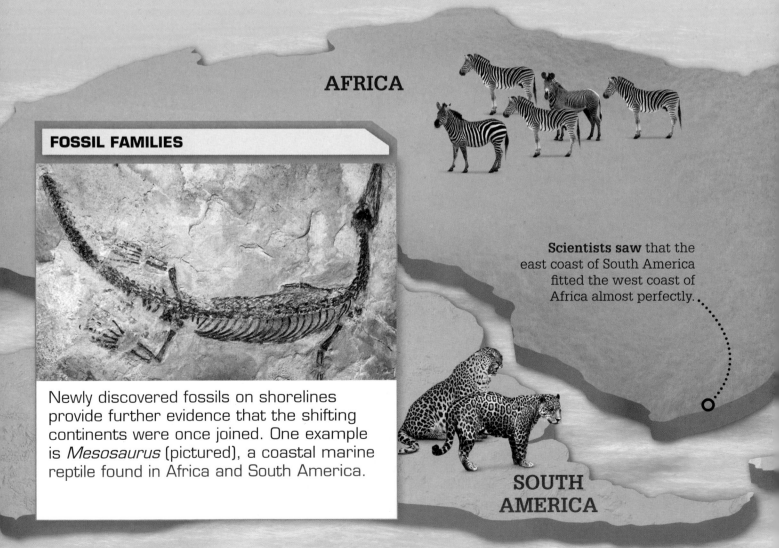

AFRICA

FOSSIL FAMILIES

Newly discovered fossils on shorelines provide further evidence that the shifting continents were once joined. One example is *Mesosaurus* (pictured), a coastal marine reptile found in Africa and South America.

Scientists saw that the east coast of South America fitted the west coast of Africa almost perfectly.

SOUTH AMERICA

FAST FACTS

PLATES MOVE APART AT DIFFERENT RATES

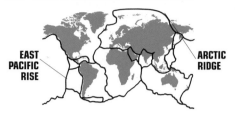

EAST PACIFIC RISE

ARCTIC RIDGE

The slowest rate of plate separation occurs at the Arctic ridge, at 2.5 cm (1 in) each year. By contrast, at the East Pacific Rise near Easter Island, the plates are moving apart at the speedy rate of more than 15 cm (6 in) each year.

MOUNT EVEREST IS GETTING TALLER

Global positioning satellite (GPS) readings suggest that Mount Everest is growing by up to 0.016 mm (0.0006 in) every day, and that the Himalaya Mountains as a whole rise by 1 cm (0.4 in) each year. This is caused by the Indian tectonic plate moving into the Eurasian plate.

SOME OF TODAY'S CONTINENTS WERE ONCE LINKED BY LAND BRIDGES

ASIA NORTH AMERICA

BERING STRAIT

These land bridges did exist for periods of time; for example, North America and Asia were linked intermittently by a land bridge over what is now the Bering Strait.

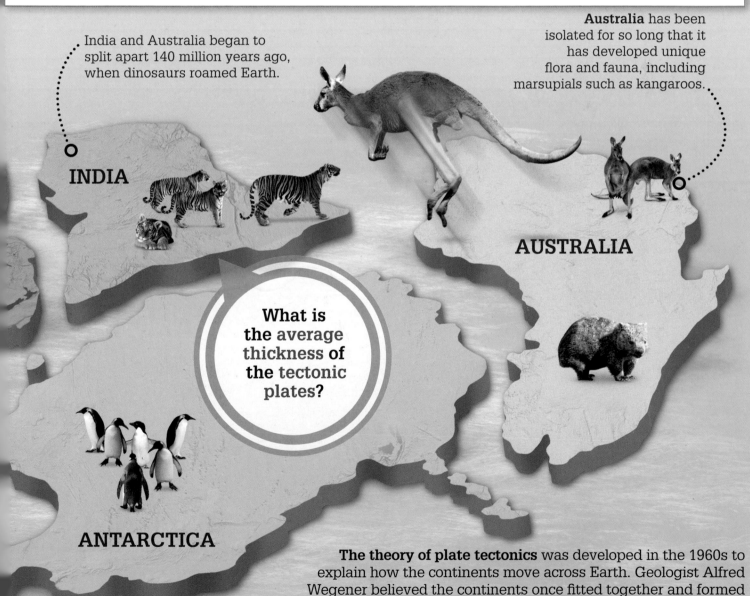

India and Australia began to split apart 140 million years ago, when dinosaurs roamed Earth.

Australia has been isolated for so long that it has developed unique flora and fauna, including marsupials such as kangaroos.

INDIA

AUSTRALIA

What is the average thickness of the tectonic plates?

ANTARCTICA

The theory of plate tectonics was developed in the 1960s to explain how the continents move across Earth. Geologist Alfred Wegener believed the continents once fitted together and formed the theory of continental drift. It is now known that Earth's top layer, the lithosphere, has cracked into seven large plates carrying the continents, with many smaller plates. Heat currents under the surface power their gradual movement.

TRUE or FALSE? There are seven seas

This expression comes from sailors thousands of years ago, but it is as **mythical as mermaids**. In truth there are **five oceans** and more than **50 seas** that make up our **saltwater world** today.

Adriatic Sea

Black Sea

Caspian Sea

Mediterranean Sea

Persian Gulf

Red Sea

Arabian Sea

DEEP DIVE

Only five per cent of the ocean has been explored, while the rest is a vast unknown. In 1960 a specially built bathyscaphe named *Trieste* descended to the Marianas Trench – the deepest point on Earth at 10,910 m (35,797 ft). The bathyscaphe resisted pressures of up to 200,000 tonnes.

NORTH AMERICA

The Atlantic Ocean is, on average, the saltiest ocean.

The Pacific Ocean is almost the same size as all the other oceans combined.

SOUTH AMERICA

The original seven seas referred to in early European and Islamic texts encompassed the Mediterranean, Adriatic, Arabian, Black, Red, Caspian, and Persian Gulf. But this was because sailors had not travelled beyond their immediate waters. Oceans and seas are often used to mean the same thing, but oceans are open expanses of water, while most seas are partly enclosed by land.

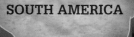

📊 FAST FACTS

OCEANS CONTAIN
97% OF EARTH'S WATER

The largest ocean, the Pacific, houses nearly half of this saltwater. The remaining 3 per cent of Earth's water is freshwater.

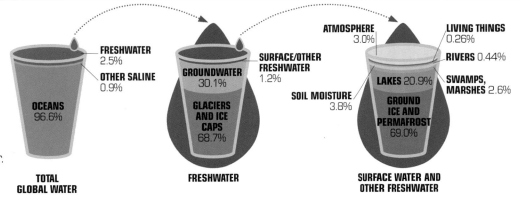

FRESHWATER
2.5%

OTHER SALINE
0.9%

OCEANS
96.6%

TOTAL GLOBAL WATER

GROUNDWATER
30.1%

SURFACE/OTHER FRESHWATER
1.2%

GLACIERS AND ICE CAPS
68.7%

FRESHWATER

ATMOSPHERE
3.0%

LIVING THINGS
0.26%

RIVERS 0.44%

LAKES 20.9%

SWAMPS, MARSHES 2.6%

SOIL MOISTURE
3.8%

GROUND ICE AND PERMAFROST
69.0%

SURFACE WATER AND OTHER FRESHWATER

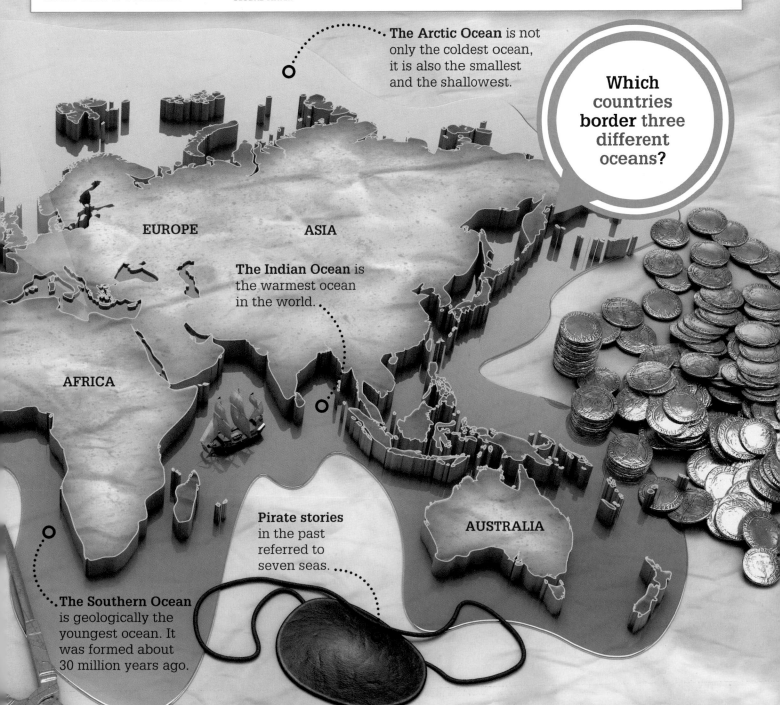

The Arctic Ocean is not only the coldest ocean, it is also the smallest and the shallowest.

Which countries border three different oceans?

EUROPE

ASIA

The Indian Ocean is the warmest ocean in the world.

AFRICA

AUSTRALIA

Pirate stories in the past referred to seven seas.

The Southern Ocean is geologically the youngest ocean. It was formed about 30 million years ago.

The Amazon River is home to an incredible variety of creatures. Species include the anaconda, river otter, and the Amazon river dolphin. There are 2,000 types of fish, more than the number in the Atlantic Ocean. The deadly piranha fish is one of them.

TRUE or FALSE?

Earth's longest river is the Amazon

The Amazon in South America is by far the largest and widest river, but it falls short in the long run. The Amazon comes a close second to the Nile in northeastern Africa.

0 km   1,000   2,000   3,000

AMAZON RIVER

Lake Victoria is the largest tropical lake in the world.

NILE RIVER

The Amazon River flows through Peru, Columbia, and Brazil.

The Nile River is named after the Greek for "river valley".

With its lakes and tributaries, the Nile connects 11 African countries, flowing northwards from Burundi to Egypt.

Thousands of tributaries (streams) flow into the main river course.

The Nile has two major tributaries: the White Nile, which originates in Burundi, and the Blue Nile, which originates

WHITE NILE

BLUE NILE

0 miles   200   400   600   800   1,000   1,200   1,400   1,600   1,800   2,0

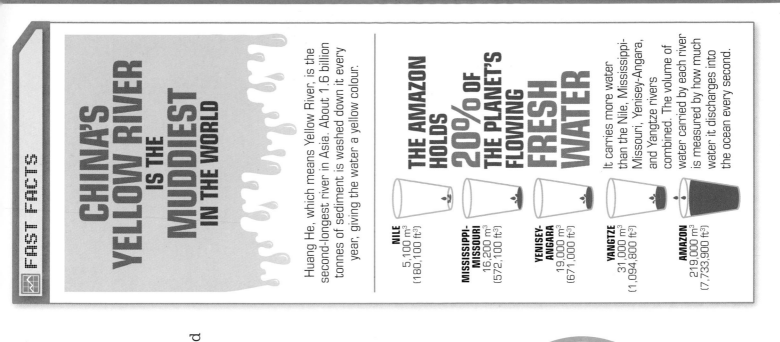

FAST FACTS

CHINA'S YELLOW RIVER IS THE MUDDIEST IN THE WORLD

Huang He, which means Yellow River, is the second-longest river in Asia. About 1.6 billion tonnes of sediment is washed down it every year, giving the water a yellow colour.

THE AMAZON HOLDS 20% OF THE PLANET'S FLOWING FRESH WATER

It carries more water than the Nile, Mississippi-Missouri, Yenisey-Angara, and Yangtze rivers combined. The volume of water carried by each river is measured by how much water it discharges into the ocean every second.

NILE
5,100 m³
(180,100 ft³)

MISSISSIPPI-MISSOURI
16,200 m³
(572,100 ft³)

YENISEY-ANGARA
19,000 m³
(671,000 ft³)

YANGTZE
31,000 m³
(1,094,800 ft³)

AMAZON
219,000 m³
(7,733,900 ft³)

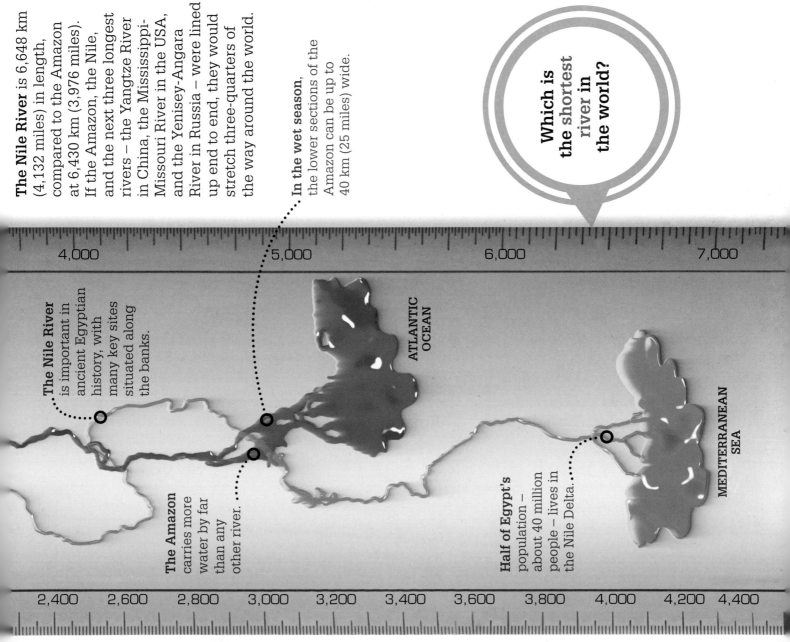

The Nile River is 6,648 km (4,132 miles) in length, compared to the Amazon at 6,430 km (3,976 miles). If the Amazon, the Nile, and the next three longest rivers – the Yangtze River in China, the Mississippi-Missouri River in the USA, and the Yenisey-Angara River in Russia – were lined up end to end, they would stretch three-quarters of the way around the world.

In the wet season, the lower sections of the Amazon can be up to 40 km (25 miles) wide.

Which is the shortest river in the world?

The Nile River is important in ancient Egyptian history, with many key sites situated along the banks.

ATLANTIC OCEAN

The Amazon carries more water by far than any other river.

Half of Egypt's population – about 40 million people – lives in the Nile Delta.

MEDITERRANEAN SEA

4,000 5,000 6,000 7,000

2,400 2,600 2,800 3,000 3,200 3,400 3,600 3,800 4,000 4,200 4,400

TRUE or FALSE?

Mount Everest is the world's tallest mountain

Everest is topped by another **mighty mound**, which is often overlooked because so much of it is **hidden under the sea**. Lesser known **Mauna Kea** triumphs over Everest easily if measured **base to peak**.

Although the top of Mauna Kea is only 4,205 m (13,796 ft) above sea level, it is the tallest mountain on Earth in total base to peak height.

FAST FACTS

As you go up a mountain, the air pressure decreases. This makes it harder to breathe because oxygen can't pass through the lungs into the blood as easily as at sea level. The body responds by making more red blood cells to carry more oxygen and keep you healthy.

PEOPLE LIVING AT HIGH ALTITUDE HAVE MORE RED BLOOD CELLS

ABOUT 70 MILLION PEOPLE LIVE IN THE HIMALAYAS

HIMALAYAS 70 million people

FRANCE 67 million people

This giant mountain range is an inhospitable place, yet a population greater than that of France lives in the Himalayas. Despite the harsh weather and lack of flat ground, most mountain communities rely on agriculture to sustain them.

MOUNTAINOUS MARS

Bigger than any mountain on our planet is Olympus Mons on Mars. Forming about three billion years ago, this shield volcano towers almost 22 km (14 miles) – more than two times higher than the tallest mountain on Earth.

Mauna Kea in Hawaii is a dormant volcano, which last erupted 4,500 years ago. Measured from its underwater base in the Pacific Ocean, it stretches 9,750 m (32,000 ft) to the top. This makes Everest in the Himalayan Mountains appear small by comparison at 8,850 m (29,035 ft).

In ideal weather conditions, it is possible to see for 160 km (100 miles) from the top of Everest.

More than 3,000 climbers have reached Mount Everest's summit.

At what **height** does **a hill** become **a mountain?**

More than one million years old, Mauna Kea is sinking slowly at a rate of 5 mm (0.25 in) a year as the sea bed sags under its heavy weight.

TRUE or FALSE? # Deserts are always hot

This fact is a lot of hot air. In reality, **deserts can blow hot or cold**. Any area that receives **less than 25 cm (10 in) of rain** a year is a desert, so there are deserts all around the world, from blazing Africa to icy Antarctica!

Temperatures in Antarctica can dip to -62°C (-80°F) but the lack of rainfall means it is still classed as desert land.

SANDS OF TIME

Deserts are expanding as time goes on because of over-farming, deforestation, and climate change. This process is called desertification. Asia's Gobi Desert is growing at a rate of 3,600 sq km (1,390 sq miles) each year.

Plants in hot deserts must survive extreme temperatures, high winds, and arid conditions. Plants like this cactus can store water in their stems, but other plants can survive only for a short period after it rains.

It is a myth that all deserts are sandy. Only 20 per cent of the world's deserts are sand.

FAST FACTS

ABOUT 40 MILLION TONNES OF **SAHARAN DUST** IS BLOWN TO THE AMAZON RAINFOREST EACH YEAR

A valley covering 0.2 per cent of the Sahara in north Africa provides 50 per cent of all the nutrient-rich dust carried on the wind into the Amazon rainforest in Brazil.

NO RAIN HAS FALLEN IN THE FRIIS HILLS OF ANTARCTICA FOR 14 MILLION YEARS

The cold temperature and strong moisture-zapping winds have resulted in these hills receiving no measurable rain or snow. Fossils show that they were once topped by a lake when Earth's climate was warmer.

Which are the hottest and coldest deserts in the world?

Deserts can never be permanently hot. Even those located in the hottest parts of the world get very cold at night without the heat of the Sun. This is why it is hard for people to live in the desert and cope with the extremes of temperature. The priority is being near a water source, so inhabitants lead a nomadic existence, moving from place to place for survival.

TRUE or FALSE? If a **volcano** does not produce **lava**, it isn't **dangerous**

This is a dangerous assumption! All volcanoes are **deadly**. Giant ash clouds, treacherous mudflows, hazardous gases, and rocky landslides are all released when they **erupt**. Another bombshell is that about **300,000 people** have been **killed by volcanoes** in the last 400 years.

Four-fifths of Earth's surface is volcanic rock, but much of it is hidden under the ocean. Liquid magma rising from deep within Earth is spewed out by volcanoes as incandescent lava. This may be accompanied by spectacular gas and ash plumes, as seen here.

MAGMA'S
- SMOKY BURGERS
- BBQ RIBS
- EXTRA HOT CHILLI

OPEN

POMPEII STATUES

The city of Pompeii in Italy was destroyed when Mount Vesuvius erupted in 79 CE. Buried under ash and rock, 20,000 citizens died. Archaeologists found remains of the victims buried in the ash and made life-like casts of them.

Along with water vapour and carbon dioxide, deadly sulphur dioxide fills the air with poisonous gas.

What was the world's largest ever volcanic eruption?

Ash clouds can cover vast areas, forming a suffocating blanket overhead.

Over time lava and ash may build up to form a cone-shaped volcanic mountain, where it breaks through a weak point in the crust.

FAST FACTS

THE LOUDEST SOUND IN RECORDED HISTORY WAS THE KRAKATOA ERUPTION

Erupting in Indonesia in 1883, the explosion reached 180 decibels and was heard up to 4,782 km (2,970 miles) away on the island of Rodrigues, near Mauritius. Sounds above 110 dB can cause lasting hearing damage if listened to for more than a minute.

VOLCANOES RANGE FROM NON-EXPLOSIVE TO MEGA-COLOSSAL

STROMBOLI
VEI 1 gentle

ST HELENS
VEI 5 paroxysmal

KRAKATOA
VEI 6 colossal

YELLOWSTONE
VEI 8 mega-colossal

The volcanic explosivity index (VEI) measures volcanoes from zero (non-explosive) to eight (mega-colossal, mass ejections, erupting about every 10,000 years). Each interval on the scale represents a ten-fold increase in criteria, such as volume of ash, eruption, cloud height, and explosivity.

90% OF ALL VOLCANIC ACTIVITY OCCURS IN THE OCEANS

90%

10%

Underwater vents or fissures in Earth's surface, called submarine volcanoes, are mostly found at ocean ridges, where tectonic plates are moving apart. They are estimated to account for 75% of magma output each year.

TRUE or FALSE? Earthquakes are very rare

Untrue – every year there are **several million earthquakes**. Most are just **wibble-wobbles**, while a handful are **earth-shattering**, causing widespread devastation.

Richter scale 6–6.9 = strong, severe, sudden movement, on average 120 a year

The rocky plates of Earth's crust move constantly, and when they meet or slide past each other, earthquakes result. These are usually slight tremors, unless the rocks either side of a plate boundary lock together, creating much deeper vibrations. In 1934, American scientist Charles Richter designed the Richter scale – a way to measure earthquakes using instruments called seismographs.

WAVES OF DESTRUCTION

A huge earthquake on the sea bed can trigger a series of catastrophic waves, called tsunamis. Travelling at speeds up to 943 kph (586 mph), they cause mass devastation on reaching land, bringing down buildings and destroying life.

Richter scale 1–4.9 = light, minor movement, more than 64,000 a year

Is there anywhere on Earth where jelly does not wobble?

THE BIGGEST EARTHQUAKE IN THE 20TH CENTURY MEASURED

9.5 ON THE RICHTER SCALE

The Great Chilean Earthquake in 1960 resulted in landslides, tsunamis, and floods. The earthquake that caused the tsunami in the Indian Ocean on 26 December 2004 measured 9.1–9.3.

MOONQUAKES OCCUR ON THE MOON

The highest a moonquake has reached is 5.5 on the Richter scale. Though earthquakes tend to be stronger, these shallow moonquakes all lasted more than 10 minutes, whereas on Earth vibrations usually last just half a minute.

Richter scale 5–5.9 = moderate, strong sudden movement, on average 800 a year

Richter scale 8+ = super, extreme movement, on average one a year

Richter scale 7–7.9 = major, very severe movement, on average 18 a year

When Earth was young, it was knocked off-kilter by a large object. Instead of rotating with a straight axis, it now spins on an axis tilted at 23.5°. As Earth orbits the Sun, it always tilts the same way. When the North Pole is tilted towards the Sun, the northern hemisphere is heated more and it is summer. At the same time the South Pole tilts away from the Sun, making the southern hemisphere cool in winter.

In June every year, Earth's North Pole is tilted towards the Sun, giving the land there continual sunshine, with the Sun never sinking below the horizon.

TRUE or FALSE? It is warm in **summer** because Earth's orbit is **closest to the Sun**

It must be **silly season** if you believe this! When it is summer one side of our planet, it is winter on the other. Earth is **furthest from the Sun** in **summer**. The changing seasons are a result of the **tilt in Earth's axis**.

FAST FACTS

EARTH'S DAYS ARE GETTING LONGER

Due to the tidal effects the Moon has on Earth, a modern day is 1.7 milliseconds longer than a century ago. In the age of the dinosaurs, about 60 million years ago, an Earth day was less than 23 hours long.

AT MIDNIGHT ON 21 JUNE IT IS LIGHT EVERYWHERE NORTH OF THE ARCTIC CIRCLE

21 June is called the Summer Solstice in the northern hemisphere and the Winter Solstice in the southern hemisphere. There are 24 hours of daylight north of the Arctic Circle and 24 hours of darkness south of the Antarctic Circle.

Though Earth is closer to the Sun at certain times of the year, the difference in distance is so minor that it would not affect the weather.

The North Pole receives no sunlight in January, experiencing 24 hours of darkness.

MONSOON SEASON

A seasonal change in the prevailing wind has dramatic consequences for southern Asia. Warm, moist air blows northeast from ocean to land in summer, bringing the wet monsoon with heavy flooding. Cool, dry air blows from land to ocean in winter. The change in wind direction comes from the differing temperatures of land and water.

Why is it warmer at the end of summer than in the middle?

TRUE or FALSE? A **red** sky at night signals **good weather**

"Red sky at night, shepherds' delight. Red sky in the morning, shepherds' warning". This well-known saying first appeared **in the Bible** to help shepherds get ready for the next day's weather, but it **still holds true** today.

📈 FAST FACTS

BIRDS ON A TELEPHONE WIRE MAY BE A SIGN OF STORMS

Flocks of migrating birds often rest on telephone wires. But if you notice a sudden increase in birds on wires, they could be taking a break to avoid a bad storm in their path.

A **HALO** AROUND THE MOON MAY MEAN A STORM IS COMING

This is caused by ice crystals forming in high clouds, which happens before a heavy rain shower. An old saying goes, "Circle around the Moon, rain or snow soon".

WEATHER WATCHING

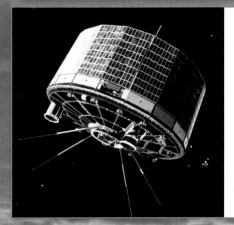

Meteorology, or the study of the atmosphere, can be traced back to India in about 3000 BCE. It took off in the 18th and 19th centuries with the invention of accurate instruments to measure weather. By the mid-20th century, satellites were circling in Space to track Earth's weather systems from the sky.

The red colour comes from dust particles in the air, and increased pollution also plays a part.

Many people believe their bodies can predict the weather. Rheumatic joints or aches from past injuries are said to be a sign of rain on the horizon.

Some cultures use the same red sky saying, but change it to "Sailors' delight" instead, depending on the people most affected by the weather.

How are seagulls said to predict the weather?

Before scientific forecasting techniques were developed, people relied on their experiences to provide accurate predictions. Red night skies indicate dust is trapped in the air by high pressure. When this moves in from the west, clear skies and sunshine are coming. Red skies in the morning suggest the good weather has moved east to be replaced by low pressure. This is a red alert, warning of rain to follow.

TRUE or FALSE? Lightning can't strike the same place twice

This may come like a **bolt from the blue**, but lightning often strikes twice. Tall targets, such as skyscrapers and trees, can be struck up to **100 times** a year. American park ranger Roy Sullivan also felt the **full force of nature** being hit **seven** times. His stroke of luck was surviving!

Each flash of forked lightning can reach up to 9 km (6 miles) from the cloud to the ground.

RETHINKING RAINDROPS

The usual depiction of a raindrop is in the classic tear shape. But small raindrops are spherical, while larger ones are more bun-shaped. As raindrops fall, they are flattened from below by air resistance. If this force exceeds the attraction of the water molecules for each other, the raindrop will split into smaller ones.

Lightning flashes are immense electric sparks that streak from the bottom to the top of a thundercloud, or from cloud-to-cloud or cloud-to-ground. The electric charges that make the sparks are created by ice crystals and water droplets crashing together in the chaotic up- and down-drafts inside the cloud.

Intense heat from the electric spark causes the air to expand and vibrate. This is heard as a thunderclap after the lightning flash.

In a split second, a bolt of lightning can heat the surrounding air to temperatures five times hotter than the Sun's surface.

Lightning is visible striking the same building in Hong Kong's central business district twice.

How can you tell if lightning is about to strike you?

FAST FACTS

YOU CAN TELL HOW FAR AWAY LIGHTNING IS BY COUNTING

+1,2,3... RUMBLE

After a lightning bolt, you can count the seconds to find out approximately how far away the lightning struck. Count the seconds between the strike and the thunder, and divide the number of seconds by 3 for distance in km, or by 5 for distance in miles.

APOLLO 12 WAS STRUCK BY LIGHTNING DURING ITS LAUNCH

Apollo 12 launched in 1969 into a rainy sky. The Saturn V rocket, was struck twice by lightning 30 seconds and 50 seconds after lift off. But because the rocket was off the ground (not earthed), no damage was caused.

LIGHTNING STRIKES ABOUT 8.6 MILLION TIMES A DAY

Each strike carries enough energy to power a city with 200,000 inhabitants for one minute. The average lightning flash would also power a 100-watt light bulb for three months.

TRUE or FALSE? No two snowflakes are the same

This fact can come in **from the cold**. At altitude, specks of dust inside clouds develop **ice crystals** that turn them into snowflakes. With at least 275 **water molecules** needed to form a small ice crystal, and at least 50 crystals in a single snowflake, each one falls to Earth in a **unique formation**.

The average snowflake has a top speed of 1.7 m (5.6 ft) a second.

Each snowflake forms its own six-sided pattern, with a change in temperature making the crystal arrangement more complex.

SNOWY SPIKES

In mountain ranges where the air is dry, such as Cerro Mercedario in Argentina, piles of snow can develop into penitentes – tall ice blades. They were first mentioned in British naturalist Charles Darwin's travel writings in 1839. Penitentes standing 5 m (16 ft) in height have since been recorded.

Snow is a form of precipitation just like rain, hail, and sleet. When flurries of flakes fall, the minimal accumulation can produce dry, new snow, called powder snow. Heavy snowfalls for prolonged periods are snowstorms. About 12 per cent of our planet is permanently covered in snow and ice.

Snow is not white, but clear and colourless.

As long as the air temperature between the cloud and ground is below 0°C (32°F), this flake will fall as snow.

The largest snowflake on record measured 38 cm (15 in) wide and 20 cm (8 in) thick in Montana, USA, in 1887.

Can it ever be too cold to snow on planet Earth?

THE WORST SNOWSTORM IN HISTORY KILLED 500 PEOPLE

In 1993 a winter storm on the eastern coast of USA wreaked havoc on the community, causing £825 million worth of damage. One meteorologist called it "a storm with the heart of a blizzard and the soul of a hurricane".

THE WORLD'S LARGEST SNOWMAN WAS A SNOWWOMAN

Built in Maine, USA, in 2008, she stood 37 m (122 ft) in height – about the same as a 12-storey building. She had trees for arms, and skis for eyelashes.

SNOW MAKES A GOOD INSULATOR

About 90% of snow is trapped air. As the air can't move, the heat loss is reduced, which makes snow a good insulator. Humans use this property to insulate igloos, and many animals keep warm by burrowing into snow to hibernate in winter.

The population of the world can fit into Los Angeles

The award for the city that can best squeeze the **global population** inside, standing shoulder to shoulder, is... **Los Angeles**. This American city can carry the **weight of the world!**

ESCAPING THE CROWDS

The least populated parts of the world are usually determined by a remote or challenging landscape, together with limited opportunities for work. This lifestyle does not appeal to everyone. Desert regions, such as the western Sahara, or isolated islands, such as Greenland (shown here), are examples.

Which country makes up one-fifth of the global population?

There are 1.01 men in the world for every woman.

Every year 137 million babies are born and 55 million people die. This means the population grows by 82 million.

Nicknamed Oscar, the gold-plated statue for the Academy Awards was first given in 1929 at a ceremony in Hollywood, Los Angeles. Thousands of winners have received them since.

Los Angeles ("City of Angels") in the USA, covers 1,300 sq km (500 sq miles). This is just enough to accommodate the seven billion people in the world – but breathe in! Tokyo in Japan is the world's most populated city with more than nine million people, while the smallest city by population is Hum in Croatia, with approximately 23 people.

FAST FACTS

THE WORLD'S POPULATION IS *GROWING* AT A RATE OF 8,760 PEOPLE AN HOUR

This means almost 150 people are added to the planet every minute. But the world is top-heavy – 90 per cent of its total population lives in the northern hemisphere.

ABOUT *108* BILLION PEOPLE HAVE LIVED ON EARTH

There are seven billion people alive at present, which means about 6.5% of all the people who ever lived are alive now.

ALIVE AT PRESENT 6.5%

8% OF THE WORLD'S POPULATION ARE OVER 65

CURRENTLY 8%

2050 25%

This will rise to 25% by 2050. Better food, healthcare, hygiene, and education have all contributed to our rising life expectancy, which has doubled in the last 200 years. It depends where you live, though – illnesses that are treatable in the West can have a devastating impact on poorer populations.

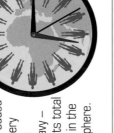

Down to Earth

BLOWN AWAY

An '**EYE**' (centre) of a hurricane can be **32 KM** (20 MILES) across – larger than **MANHATTAN**, New York, USA.

HURRICANE WINDS CAN REACH SPEEDS OF 300 KPH (186 MPH).

FROGS poured down from the sky in Kansas City, USA, in 1873, and **HERRING** fell on a group of golfers in Bournemouth, UK, in 1948. These creatures had been *swept into the clouds* by wind and dropped into different locations.

EARTH THROUGH THE AGES

5,000 MYA	4,000 MYA	3,000 MYA

FORMATION OF EARTH
4,540 MYA

FORMATION OF THE MOON
c **4,500** MYA

FIRST LIFE
3,800 MYA

HIGH LIFE

Seven highest peaks on the seven continents

MOUNT EVEREST – Asia
8,850 m (29,035 ft)

ACONCAGUA – South America
6,960 m (22,838 ft)

MOUNT MCKINLEY – North America
6,194 m (20,322 ft)

KILIMANJARO – Africa
5,895 m (19,340 ft)

MOUNT ELBRUS – Europe
5,642 m (18,510 ft)

VINSON MASSIF – Antarctica
4,897 m (16,066 ft)

PUNCAK JAYA – Australasia
4,884 m (16,023 ft)

In 2005 Davo Karnicar became the first person to **SKI** down *Mount Everest*.

MAKING A SPLASH

SOUTH AMERICA **ANGEL FALLS – Venezuela**
979 m (3,212 ft)

AFRICA **TUGELA FALLS – South Africa**
948 m (3,110 ft)

AUSTRALASIA **OLO'UPENA FALLS – Hawaii**
900 m (2,953 ft)

EUROPE **VINNUFALLET – Norway**
865 m (2,837 ft)

NORTH AMERICA **JAMES BRUCE FALLS – Canada**
840 m (2,755 ft)

ASIA **HANNOKI-NO-TAKI – Japan**
500 m (1,640 ft)

In **1901** American Annie Taylor became the first person to go over Niagara Falls in a barrel – she survived!

The tallest waterfall in each continent (except for Antarctica)

2,000 MYA   1000 MYA

IF ALL OF **EARTH'S HISTORY** TOOK PLACE IN A **SINGLE YEAR,** HUMANS WOULDN'T APPEAR UNTIL **25 MINUTES** BEFORE MIDNIGHT ON NEW YEAR'S EVE.

FIRST DINOSAURS
245 MYA

MODERN HUMANS
200,000 YEARS AGO

DEADLY ERUPTIONS

1902
Mount Pelée,
Martinique
30,000

CE **79**
Mount Vesuvius,
Italy
20,000

1985
Nevado del Ruiz,
Columbia
25,000

1815
Mount Tambora,
Indonesia
92,000

1883
Mount Krakatoa,
Indonesia
36,000

Eruptions that have killed tens of thousands of people

DELVING DEEP

Diamond is Earth's hardest natural material, and is used for cutting other hard substances. Today's diamond use is:

70%
INDUSTRY

30%
JEWELLERY

Emeralds, rubies, and sapphires are all more rare than diamonds.

History and culture

Let's delve deep into the past and explore ancient civilizations, cultural traditions, and key events that have shaped the world today. But what is fact and what is fabrication is often blurred by the mists of time. Read on to make all the hype and humbug history.

This ancient Greek temple on the Acropolis in Athens is called the Erechtheion. Its porch is supported not by columns, but by female figures cast in stone and clad in simple tunics. These lovely ladies are known as caryatids.

TRUE or FALSE? Neanderthals were really hairy and talked in grunts

This unflattering description comes from **media stereotypes** of early peoples. Science reveals Neanderthals were not overly hairy and talked similarly to people today. **DNA** studies show they were a **separate evolutionary line** to humans, dying out 30,000 years ago.

GENOME PROJECTS

The Human Genome Project involved scientists mapping more than 20,000 genes that make human DNA (shown) – the design for life. Then it was the turn of the Neanderthal Genome Project, using genetic material (or DNA) extracted from fossil bones. It is now possible to clone a Neanderthal and bring it to life, though this would be costly and open to ethical debate.

They hunted prey with spears and used a range of stone tools to cut up carcasses.

The icy climate about 200,000 years ago was tough. Neanderthal noses were bigger to warm the cold air.

Computer models show that if Neanderthals had been really hairy, they would have sweated excessively. This sweat would have frozen, bringing the risk of death by hypothermia. The notion of grunting was also dispelled by scientists in 1983 when a Neanderthal hyoid bone (part of the vocal system) was found in a cave in Israel. Identical to a human one, it proved their capacity for speech resembled our own.

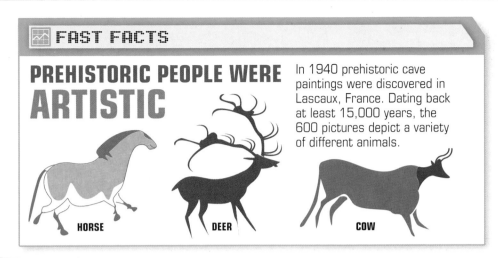

FAST FACTS

PREHISTORIC PEOPLE WERE ARTISTIC

In 1940 prehistoric cave paintings were discovered in Lascaux, France. Dating back at least 15,000 years, the 600 pictures depict a variety of different animals.

HORSE

DEER

COW

Neanderthals were very strong and powerful, though much shorter and more heavily built than humans today.

How do we know Neanderthals enjoyed music?

Cave dwellings were strengthened with branches and bones, and covered in animal skins.

Neanderthals did not hunch over like chimps, but walked upright like humans.

TRUE or FALSE? The **pyramids** were built by slaves

One of the **seven wonders** of the world, the **Great Pyramid** at Giza was slaved over by a workforce of willing men from **all walks of life**. Rather than a cruel endeavour on the orders of the Pharaoh, it was a **labour of love** for the community.

The King's chamber is the actual burial room, which is lined with granite.

This abandoned burial chamber was mistakenly named the Queen's chamber by early explorers.

Original burial chamber is carved into bedrock.

PRESERVATION PROCESS

In ancient Egypt the bodies of the deceased were preserved by mummification. This process was meant to take them safely to the afterlife. Internal organs were cut out, dried, and wrapped in linen before being stored in special containers called canopic jars (above).

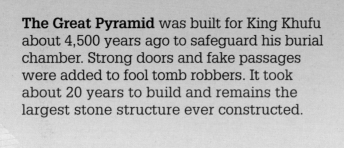

The Great Pyramid was built for King Khufu about 4,500 years ago to safeguard his burial chamber. Strong doors and fake passages were added to fool tomb robbers. It took about 20 years to build and remains the largest stone structure ever constructed.

The pyramid stands 138 m (450 ft) in height and weighs 6.5 million tonnes.

Five cavities spread the immense weight of the stones above.

How many stone blocks were used to build the Great Pyramid?

The grand gallery is 9 m (28 ft) high, 47 m (153 ft) long, and only 2 m (7 ft) wide.

The original hidden entrance is 17 m (56 ft) above the ground.

Escape shaft

📊 **FAST FACTS**

THE SPHINX WATCHES OVER THE DEAD

With the body of a lion and the head of a human (usually a pharaoh), an Egyptian sphinx was a guardian figure. The Great Sphinx was built in stone at the front of the Great Pyramid.

EGYPTIANS WROTE IN PICTURES

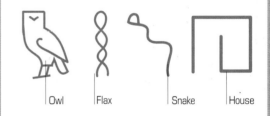

| Owl | Flax | Snake | House |

These pictures are called hieroglyphs, and each one represents a word, syllable, or sound. Hieroglyphs could be read from left to right or from right to left, depending on which way the pictures were facing.

Shiny, white limestone slabs covered the surface of the pyramid and concealed the bricks underneath.

Craftsmen and labourers worked intensively as part of a state building project for set periods of time without paying taxes.

TRUE or FALSE? Greek statues are white **marble**

The classical world was home to **true masters of art**. They pioneered developments in painting and sculpting, leaving a legacy of **fine work** behind. But the white marble statues we associate with Greece are a bit **off-colour**. The originals were really **brightly painted**. It is just that the pigments have **worn away** over time.

According to ancient Greek artists, statues left plain were considered ugly.

GREEK DRAMA

Most ancient Greek cities had a theatre because plays were part of religious festivals. Crowds of up to 18,000 people would gather in the open air to watch the drama on stage. Only men and boys were allowed to act, and they wore masks to express character and feelings.

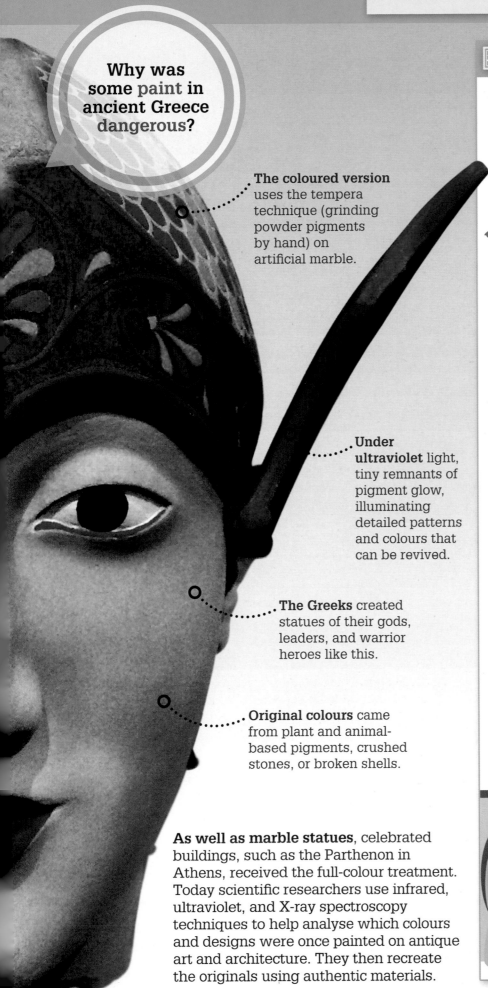

Why was some paint in ancient Greece dangerous?

The coloured version uses the tempera technique (grinding powder pigments by hand) on artificial marble.

Under ultraviolet light, tiny remnants of pigment glow, illuminating detailed patterns and colours that can be revived.

The Greeks created statues of their gods, leaders, and warrior heroes like this.

Original colours came from plant and animal-based pigments, crushed stones, or broken shells.

As well as marble statues, celebrated buildings, such as the Parthenon in Athens, received the full-colour treatment. Today scientific researchers use infrared, ultraviolet, and X-ray spectroscopy techniques to help analyse which colours and designs were once painted on antique art and architecture. They then recreate the originals using authentic materials.

FAST FACTS

ANCIENT GREECE
WAS NOT A NATION

Instead, it was a collection of city-states, each with its own way of governing and waging wars. But although the city-states competed with one another, their inhabitants spoke the same language and worshipped the same gods.

BEANS WERE OFF
THE MENU

Unlike most modern vegetarians, some ancient Greeks, led by the philosopher and mathematician Pythagoras, refused to eat – or even touch – beans. They believed that beans contained the souls of the dead.

CRETE HAD
FLUSHING LOOS

Home to the ancient Minoans, the Greek city-state of Crete was the first place to have flushing toilets. In the palace of Knossos, water was poured into the lavatory from storage tanks to wash away royal deposits.

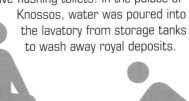

Drain

Water channel

TRUE or FALSE? Roman Emperors signalled thumbs up to save a gladiator

Bloodthirsty battles between **trained fighters** called **gladiators** took place in the **huge arenas** of ancient Rome. There was **no rule of thumb** though. The Emperor held the gladiators' lives in the palm of his hand. An **open palm** meant "**Spare him**", while a closed one ordered "**Kill him**".

The word "gladiator" comes from the Latin for "sword". ·············

ROMULUS AND REMUS

The city of Rome was founded in 753 BCE by its first king, Romulus. Legend tells that Romulus had a twin named Remus. Abandoned as babies, a she-wolf raised them in the wild. When they grew into men, Romulus killed Remus in a battle to become Rome's sole ruler.

Slaves and criminals were usually chosen as gladiators because they had nothing to lose. Trained in special schools called ludi, they learned how to use different weapons. Gladiators often fought in pairs. Death rates were high, though some gladiators survived more than 50 combats. Other fighters battled wild animals such as lions or bears.

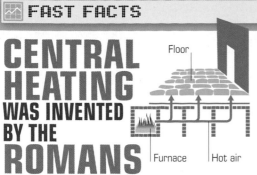

FAST FACTS

CENTRAL HEATING WAS INVENTED BY THE ROMANS

Floor · Furnace · Hot air

The comfort-loving Romans were a skilful bunch. Not only did they install underfloor heating in their homes and public buildings, they also invented cement and built the first proper roads – and very straight they were, too.

DURING A LIFE IN SERVICE, AN AVERAGE ROMAN SOLDIER MARCHED 365,000 KM (226,800 MILES)

x9

That amounts to walking around the world nine times! Soldiers were all male Roman citizens, aged 20 or older, and they weren't allowed to get married. They had to serve for 25 years.

THE ROMANS ATE ROASTED PARROT

They also tucked into such exotic delicacies as dormice, stork, flamingo, lark's tongue, and sea urchins. Ingredients were shipped to Rome from all over the empire.

If a gladiator killed his opponent before the Emperor gave his permission, the gladiator would be put on trial for murder.

The Colosseum in Rome held the largest gladiator games, in front of more than 50,000 spectators.

On special occasions, as a mark of his status, the Emperor wore a laurel wreath – the Roman symbol of victory.

What was special about the colour purple in ancient Rome?

TRUE or FALSE? Vikings wore horned helmets

Experts once **locked horns** on this subject, but it is now known that Viking helmets were **conical-shaped**. If horned helmets ever existed, they were only used for **ceremonial purposes**.

Which popular winter sport was enjoyed by the Vikings?

The Vikings were farmers-turned-raiders from Denmark, Norway, and Sweden. From the 790s onwards, they invaded Britain, Ireland, and France, causing chaos as they conquered. Some Vikings travelled to Iceland and Greenland where they set up colonies, while others navigated the rivers of Russia to trade with the Arab and Byzantine empires.

Instead of horned helmets, Vikings usually opted for basic leather and metal-frame helmets or just went bareheaded.

The idea of horned helmets came from the 19th century when idealized paintings of the Vikings grew popular.

The freezing cold Scandinavian winters would have made fur hats far more practical than horned ones.

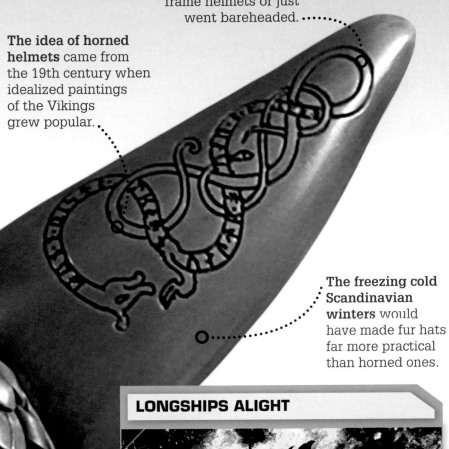

FAST FACTS

VIKINGS BATHED ONCE A WEEK

SCRAPER

COMB

TWEEZERS

As a result, these fearsome warriors were much cleaner than other Europeans at the time. Excavations of Viking settlements have uncovered tools for personal hygiene crafted from animal bones and antlers.

THOR WAS THE VIKING GOD OF THUNDER

He had a magic belt, iron gloves, and a hammer. The Vikings had their own pagan religion, and worshipped many gods. Their tales of gods, giants, monsters, and elves are known as the Norse myths.

VIKING RUNES HAD MAGICAL PROPERTIES

A R M B S T

The Vikings used an alphabet of 16 symbols called runes to label their belongings, decorate gravestones, or write poems. Discovered by the god Odin, runes were said to have special powers, but only rune masters could cast spells or curses.

LONGSHIPS ALIGHT

Vikings travelled in longships, or dragon-ships, decorated with fearsome, carved animal heads. These shallow oar- and wind-powered vessels were fast and strong enough to cross the stormy Atlantic Ocean. Dead Viking leaders may have been cremated inside their ships.

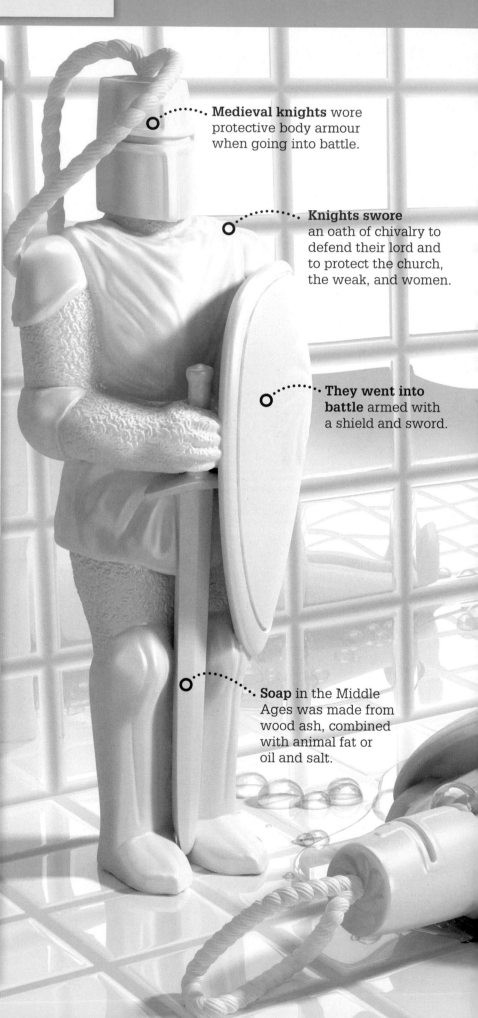

MEDIEVAL PEOPLE USED
SLICES OF BREAD
AS PLATES

They weren't a very well-mannered lot, by modern standards. They ate with knives and fingers, rather than forks, and threw their chewed bones on the floor. Still, at least there wasn't much washing up to do!

WOOL WAS WASHED IN WEE

Before a greasy, grubby fleece could be turned into wool, it had to be washed. The most effective way to do this was to scrub it in urine diluted with water.

A GRAND HOUSEHOLD COULD BURN
45 kg (100 lb) OF WAX
AND TALLOW IN A SINGLE NIGHT

The equivalent of 1,300 candles, this might be used to light a lavish banquet in a dark medieval castle, at which swans and peacocks were served, feathers and all.

Medieval knights wore protective body armour when going into battle.

Knights swore an oath of chivalry to defend their lord and to protect the church, the weak, and women.

They went into battle armed with a shield and sword.

Soap in the Middle Ages was made from wood ash, combined with animal fat or oil and salt.

TRUE or FALSE? Medieval people didn't wash

This is just a **dirty lie**. Medieval people were **clean-living** folk, washing their hands before and after meals. Soap was so popular by the 13th century that it was produced on an **industrial scale** in Britain, France, Italy, and Spain.

Medieval life was based on a feudal system, in which land was given in exchange for service. The King was at the top, passing land to his noblemen, who provided soldiers in return. These were knights (pictured) who fought on horseback. Many won prestige and recognition in battle. At the bottom were the peasants who farmed the land, keeping a share of the harvest for themselves.

What did most people drink in the Middle Ages?

ROUTE TO KNIGHTHOOD

The sons of noblemen started training for knighthood from the age of seven. Known as pages, the boys learned how to fight and ride into battle. At 15 years old, they were assigned knights to serve, and became squires. Intensive "on the job" training was given until they were ready for the special ceremony in which they became knights themselves.

TRUE or FALSE?

Rats spread the Plague

For centuries, we've been blaming these rodents for one of history's **worst diseases**. The Plague or **the Black Death** of the 1340s killed **half the population** of Europe and millions more in Asia and Africa. Eventually it was discovered that **fleas on rats** were the true cause, but rats still played their part in **spreading the disease**.

What did people do to stop the Plague spreading that made it worse?

HEALTH AND HYGIENE

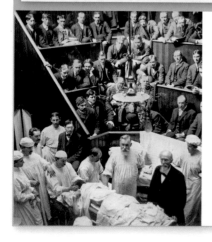

In the 1860s the medical industry at last focused on hygiene and sanitation to improve healthcare standards. Surgeons washed their hands to prevent infection and cleaned wounds with carbolic acid to kill bacteria. Sewers were built to prevent bacteria from human waste polluting drinking water.

People believed they could catch the Plague by breathing bad air. In reality, the true cause of the disease was bacteria, passed on by flea bites. Sufferers tried in vain to find cures, such as drinking urine, spreading butter on their sores, or putting toads on them.

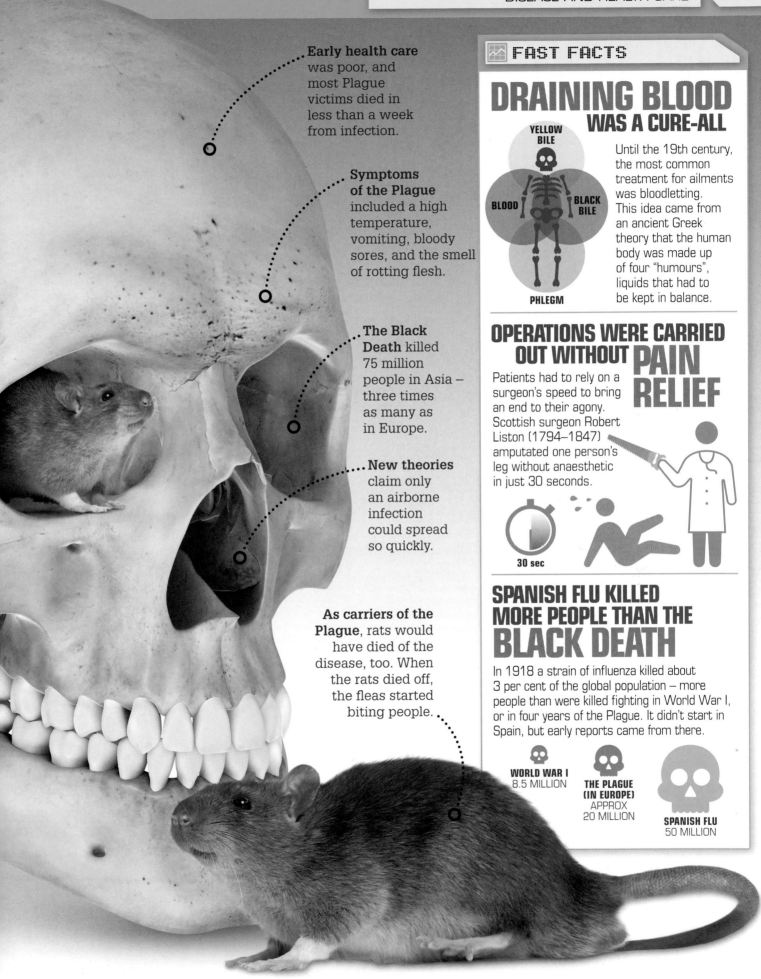

Early health care was poor, and most Plague victims died in less than a week from infection.

Symptoms of the Plague included a high temperature, vomiting, bloody sores, and the smell of rotting flesh.

The Black Death killed 75 million people in Asia – three times as many as in Europe.

New theories claim only an airborne infection could spread so quickly.

As carriers of the Plague, rats would have died of the disease, too. When the rats died off, the fleas started biting people.

FAST FACTS

DRAINING BLOOD
WAS A CURE-ALL

YELLOW BILE

BLOOD

BLACK BILE

PHLEGM

Until the 19th century, the most common treatment for ailments was bloodletting. This idea came from an ancient Greek theory that the human body was made up of four "humours", liquids that had to be kept in balance.

OPERATIONS WERE CARRIED OUT WITHOUT PAIN RELIEF

Patients had to rely on a surgeon's speed to bring an end to their agony. Scottish surgeon Robert Liston (1794–1847) amputated one person's leg without anaesthetic in just 30 seconds.

30 sec

SPANISH FLU KILLED MORE PEOPLE THAN THE BLACK DEATH

In 1918 a strain of influenza killed about 3 per cent of the global population – more people than were killed fighting in World War I, or in four years of the Plague. It didn't start in Spain, but early reports came from there.

WORLD WAR I
8.5 MILLION

THE PLAGUE (IN EUROPE)
APPROX 20 MILLION

SPANISH FLU
50 MILLION

TRUE or FALSE? Columbus discovered America

In 1492 Christopher Columbus **sailed west** from Spain looking for Asia. He landed in the Bahamas on a journey that **opened up the Americas** to other explorers. But someone always gets there first! Native people were inhabiting the **New World**, and a Viking had **pipped him to the post** 500 years before.

EXOTIC GOODS

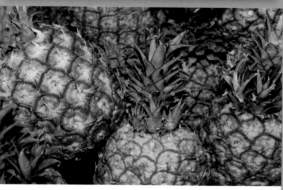

During the great age of exploration, European travellers returned with a growing menu of new foods. Potatoes, tomatoes, pineapples, and cocoa were introduced from the New World. Asian spices were so valuable in the 15th century that they were used as currency.

Columbus landed on an island in what is now the Bahamas, and called it San Salvador.

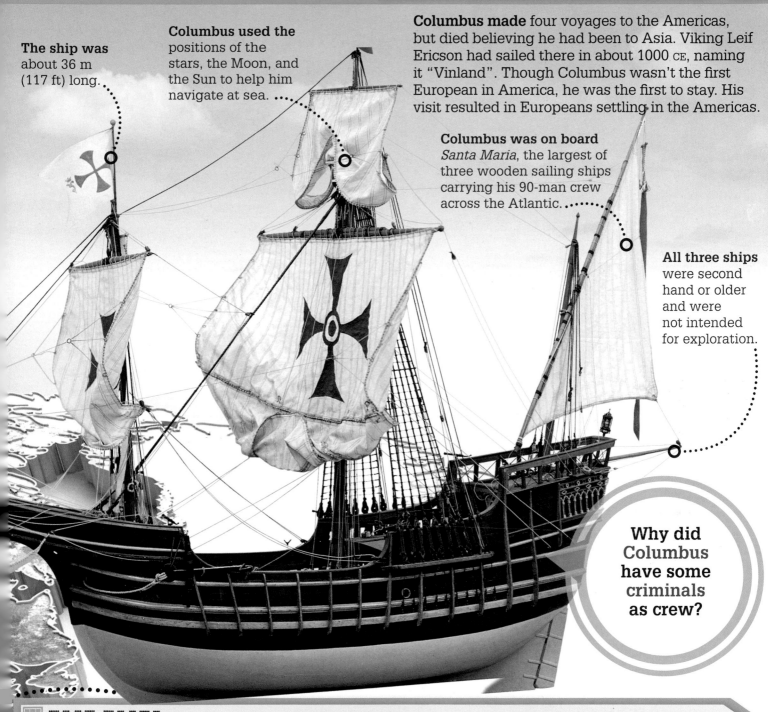

The ship was about 36 m (117 ft) long.

Columbus used the positions of the stars, the Moon, and the Sun to help him navigate at sea.

Columbus made four voyages to the Americas, but died believing he had been to Asia. Viking Leif Ericson had sailed there in about 1000 CE, naming it "Vinland". Though Columbus wasn't the first European in America, he was the first to stay. His visit resulted in Europeans settling in the Americas.

Columbus was on board *Santa Maria*, the largest of three wooden sailing ships carrying his 90-man crew across the Atlantic.

All three ships were second hand or older and were not intended for exploration.

Why did Columbus have some criminals as crew?

📈 FAST FACTS

BRAZIL WAS DISCOVERED BY ACCIDENT

Portuguese explorer Pedro Alvares Cabral stumbled across the country on his way to India in 1500. This explains why Brazilians speak Portuguese, while Spanish is spoken in most other South American countries.

LANGUAGES
SPANISH
PORTUGUESE
ENGLISH
DUTCH
FRENCH

EUROPEAN DISEASES WIPED OUT THE LOCALS

The Spanish soldiers not only imported horses, cattle, pigs, wheat, and guns to Central America. They also brought deadly European diseases such as smallpox, which had a devastating effect on native populations.

NATIVE POPULATION OF CENTRAL AMERICA

POPULATION IN 1519
25 MILLION

POPULATION IN 1565
2.5 MILLION

EXPLORATION WAS A RISKY BUSINESS

92.4% DIED

7.6% SURVIVED

In 1519 Portuguese explorer Ferdinand Magellan set sail around the world with a crew of 237. Only 18 survived the voyage. Magellan himself was killed in the Philippines after becoming embroiled in a battle between local chieftains.

TRUE or FALSE?

Marie Antoinette said, "Let them eat cake!"

Against a background of revolution (1789–99), the **French Queen** was said to have mocked **poor peasants** who wanted bread, but there is no supporting evidence. Historians insist Marie Antoinette was **kind** and **giving**. It is possible that anti-royalists made up stories to give the royal family a **bad press** at a turbulent time.

Marie Antoinette was only 14 years old when she was crowned queen, and became well-known for her beauty and flamboyant nature — she came to epitomize all that was wrong with the monarchy.

FAST FACTS

THE FRENCH HELPED TO FUND THE AMERICAN REVOLUTION (1775 – 83)

In 1775, 14 years before the French Revolution began, 13 colonies in America rebelled against British rule. The resulting war saw the creation of the USA. The modern US flag has 50 stars for the 50 states and 13 stripes for the original colonies.

Stars represent US states

Stripes represent rebellious colonies

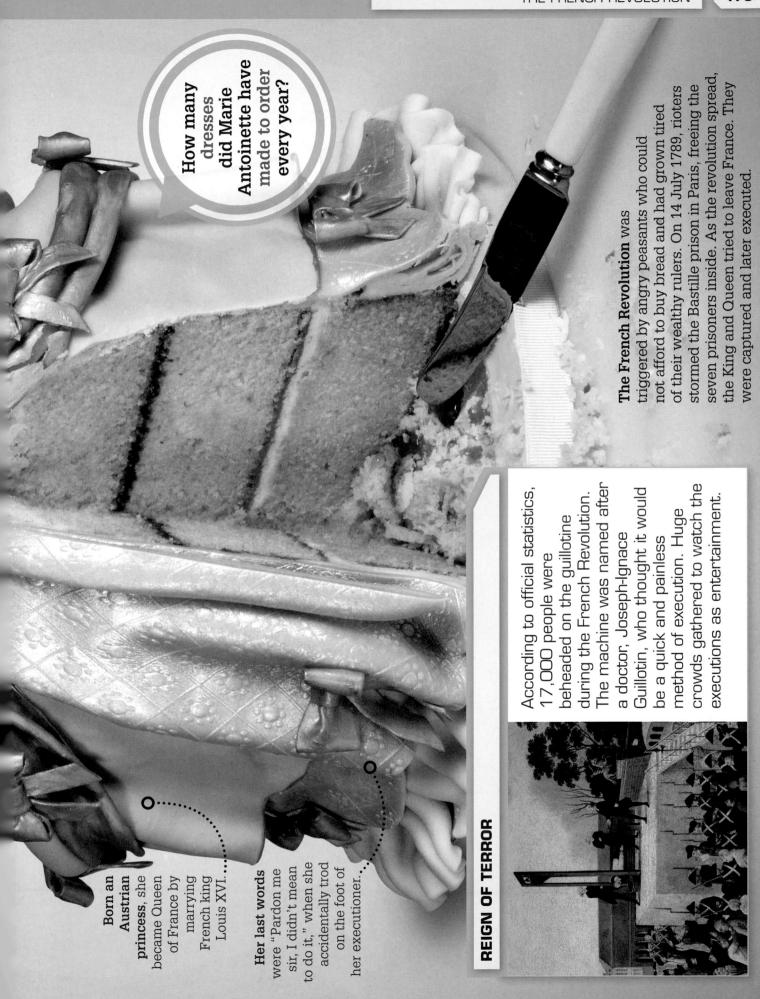

How many dresses did Marie Antoinette have made to order every year?

The French Revolution was triggered by angry peasants who could not afford to buy bread and had grown tired of their wealthy rulers. On 14 July 1789, rioters stormed the Bastille prison in Paris, freeing the seven prisoners inside. As the revolution spread, the King and Queen tried to leave France. They were captured and later executed.

Born an Austrian princess, she became Queen of France by marrying French king Louis XVI.

Her last words were "Pardon me sir, I didn't mean to do it," when she accidentally trod on the foot of her executioner.

REIGN OF TERROR

According to official statistics, 17,000 people were beheaded on the guillotine during the French Revolution. The machine was named after a doctor, Joseph-Ignace Guillotin, who thought it would be a quick and painless method of execution. Huge crowds gathered to watch the executions as entertainment.

TRUE or FALSE? Napoleon was short

This one is a **tall story**, with no truth to it. The famous French leader was of **average height** for a European man in the 1800s. His men called him "**le petit caporal**" (the little corporal), but this was not meant to make him feel small. Instead, it was a **term of endearment** towards their emperor.

Which of these leaders has a prehistoric creature named after them?

Left-hander Napoleon made his army march on the right so he could brandish his sword freely at approaching traffic – most European countries still drive on the right.

It is possible that Napoleon appeared shorter than 1.7 m (5'6") because his guardsmen had to be at least 1.8 m (6'0"). They also wore tall bearskin caps, adding 46 cm (18 in) to their height. Throughout history, leaders have lined up in all different sizes, from towering President Abraham Lincoln to tiny Queen Victoria.

MONEY MATTERS

Portraits of leaders have been used to gain influence throughout history. In ancient Roman times, the Emperor was depicted as a god on coins to boost his status, from the time of Augustus until the end of the empire. Today the heads of monarchs and influential people feature on national coins and notes.

The average height of a French leader today is 1.75 m (5'9"), not much bigger than Napoleon.

FAST FACTS

MONGOL EMPIRE

GENGHIS KHAN OWNED 800 FALCONS

But falconry was not his favourite sport. This fierce warrior loved nothing more than crushing his enemies, robbing them of their wealth, riding their horses, and running off with their wives.

THE OUTSIDE OF THE WHITE HOUSE NEEDS 2,591 LITRES (570 GALLONS) OF PAINT

Sprucing up the home of the US president is a costly business. George Washington chose the spot for the presidential palace, but he never got to live there. The first president to occupy the White House was John Adams.

2 m (6'6")
1.8 m (6'0")
1.7 m (5'6")
1.5 m (5'0")
1.4 m (4'6")
1.2 m (4'0")
1.09 m (3'6")
0.9 m (3'0")

Nationalist leader Mahatma Gandhi refused to use violence in campaigning for India's independence from British rule.

Queen Victoria was one of the world's longest-reigning monarchs, ruling Great Britain for more than 63 years.

The first black President of South Africa, Nelson Mandela was in prison for 27 years for trying to overthrow the previous government.

Before becoming US President, Abraham Lincoln was an excellent wrestler who fought in hundreds of matches.

TRUE or FALSE? Enemy soldiers played football in the trenches

World War I was one of the most devastating conflicts in history, but from the **horrors of war** emerged an incredible **story of peace**. On Christmas Day 1914, troops from both sides played **football in the trenches** near Ypres, Belgium.

Poppies have been the symbol of remembrance since World War I. Canadian surgeon John McCrae wrote his poem "In Flanders fields" in 1915, describing poppies growing where soldiers died.

WARTIME DIARY

In World War II, a Jewish girl named Anne Frank kept a diary of her time hiding from the Nazis in a concealed Netherlands apartment. The Nazis found the family in 1944 and Anne died in a concentration camp. Her writing captures the hopes and fears of a child caught up in conflict and has since been read by millions.

What was the average life expectancy in the trenches of World War I?

Most of the games were played by soldiers on the same side, but a few matches involved British and German soldiers. About 10,000 soldiers took part in the unofficial Christmas Truce, also singing songs, lighting candles, and exchanging presents. As the war went on, commanders banned the truces. There are examples of similar camaraderie amid the conflicts of the Crimean, Boer, and American Civil Wars.

Trench warfare involved World War I armies facing each other from trenches dug a short distance apart, protected by coils of barbed wire.

65 MILLION MEN FOUGHT IN WORLD WAR I

This truly was a world war – troops came from 30 different countries. Germany had the greatest military strength at the outset, but suffered the highest number of fatalities.

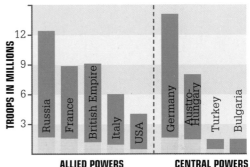

■ MILITARY STRENGTH   ☐ FATALITIES

PARACHUTING PIGEONS WERE USED IN WORLD WAR II

About 250,000 pigeons were employed in the conflict, many of which were parachuted behind enemy lines. The idea was that Resistance fighters opposed to the Nazis would send the pigeons back with secret information.

Only 1,842 pigeons returned.

TRUE or FALSE? Olympic gold medals are solid gold

All that glitters is not gold, and the Olympic medals are no exception. The last time the winners' medals were solid gold was at the Swedish games in 1912. It's been **fool's gold** ever since.

COPPER
7.5%

STERLING
SILVER
92.5%

SILVER

GOLD
1.34%

COPPER
6.16%

GOLD

OLYMPIC FLAME

The ancient Greeks lit a sacred fire during their Olympic Games. In 1936 a burning torch was carried into the arena at the modern Olympics in Berlin, Germany. Ever since, runners bring a torch lit at the ancient site of Olympia to the Games to ignite a flame that burns until the closing ceremony.

What was different about the Olympics in ancient Greece?

Silver and bronze did not exist in the ancient Olympics. There was only one winner per event, crowned with an olive wreath from a sacred tree near the temple of Zeus at Olympia.

US swimmer Michael Phelps has won 18 gold medals. The most ever won by a single person, this is double the number won by the second highest record holders.

At the ancient Olympics, winners did not receive medals. Instead, they were crowned with the kotinos, a wreath of olive leaves taken from a sacred tree. Winners' medals were first introduced at the 1904 Olympics, held in St Louis, USA. As the price of gold rose after World War I and the economic depression, the amount used in the winners' medals declined. Today there must be at least 6 grammes (0.2 oz) of gold in each gold medal.

STERLING SILVER 92.5%

ZINC AND TIN 3%

COPPER 97%

BRONZE

In 1914 Frenchman Pierre de Coubertin designed the Olympic symbol of five linked rings to represent the continents taking part.

FAST FACTS

FOOTBALL IS THE BIGGEST SPECTATOR SPORT

FOOTBALL 3.4 billion fans

FOOTBALL 2.5 billion fans

FOOTBALL 2.5 billion fans

This popular Olympic sport is an energetic business, and players can run up to 10 km (6 miles) in just one game. Perhaps this explains why the world's largest participant sport is the rather less strenuous fishing.

IN *PELOTA* THE BALL CAN MOVE AT UP TO 300 KM/H (185 MPH)

Pelota is Spanish for "ball", and this fiery game from the Basque region of the Pyrenees keeps players on their toes. They use a glove or bat, and a ball with a rubber core. It was played as an Olympic sport at the 1900 Games.

GOLF HAS BEEN PLAYED ON THE MOON

On 6 February 1971 Alan Shepard hit a golf ball on the lunar surface, having smuggled the ball and club on board in his spacesuit. Golf is due to be reinstated as an Olympic sport at the 2016 Rio Games.

TRUE or FALSE?

Hamburgers were invented in Hamburg

So many people have claimed credit for this **fast food favourite** that it has become a **bun fight**. It is known, however, that the hamburger was first sold in **the USA**, not Germany. The world soon got **a taste for it** and hamburgers haven't stopped selling since.

The "**Hamburg steak**" was a 19th-century minced beef dish served in New York, USA, to German immigrants.

STORY OF THE SANDWICH

Another popular snack – the sandwich – also has confused origins. John Montagu, fourth Earl of Sandwich, did not invent sandwiches, but they were named after him. The Earl enjoyed sandwiches as he could eat and play cards without getting sticky fingers. But Arabs had been putting meat inside pitta bread a long time previously.

The German city of Hamburg became famous for its tasty beef patties in the 19th century, but they were not placed inside buns. It is thought the first true burger was sold in 1900 by Danish immigrant Louis Lassen in Connecticut, USA. Another rumour has it that sailors from Hamburg named the meat sandwich, while others claim the name comes from Hamburg, a town in New York.

In 2012 the record for biggest burger was set in Minnesota, USA, by a bacon cheeseburger weighing 914 kg (2,014 lb).

A rice bun is used instead of bread at fast food restaurants in many Asian countries.

It is estimated that nearly 50 billion burgers are consumed every year in the USA.

Which is the world's most expensive burger?

FAST FACTS

IN INDIA IT IS RUDE

TO EAT WITH YOUR LEFT HAND

Indians spurn cutlery because they like to feel a spiritual connection with their food. So, relish your rice and devour your dal, but don't use your left hand – it is considered "unclean" and should be reserved for less appetizing activities.

NEVER STAND CHOPSTICKS UPRIGHT IN A BOWL OF FOOD

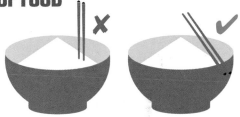

In Asia this reminds people of the incense sticks that are burned when someone dies. Instead, you should leave your chopsticks side by side. On the plus side, it's fine to slurp your soup or burp noisily once you've finished.

TERMITES MAKE A NUTRITIOUS SNACK

Insects such as termites, crickets, and caterpillars are a popular part of the menu in Africa and parts of Asia. Meanwhile, Sardinians are big fans of *casu marzu*, a local cheese that is infested with live maggots.

CRICKETS	CATERPILLARS	TERMITES
562*	370*	613*

*CALORIES PER 100 g (3.5 oz) SERVING

Listening to classical music makes you clever

Music to the ears of parents everywhere, a study in 1993 claimed teenagers who listened to Mozart **performed better** in tests.

The composer's work was played to children in the hope of producing **brainboxes**, but later reports found the **brain boost** was only **a temporary** one.

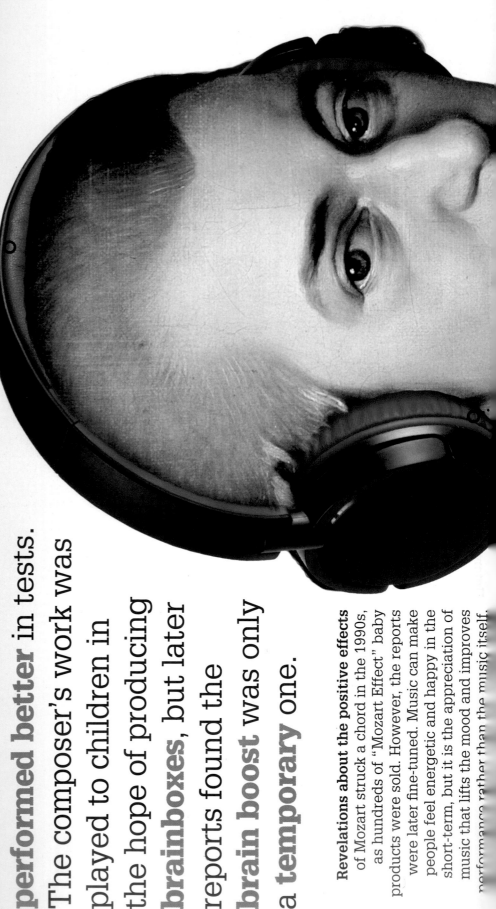

MRI scans of musicians who began playing at a young age show a larger nerve-fibre tract between the hemispheres of the brain. Learning music may increase the connections inside the brain.

Revelations about the positive effects of Mozart struck a chord in the 1990s, as hundreds of "Mozart Effect" baby products were sold. However, the reports were later fine-tuned. Music can make people feel energetic and happy in the short-term, but it is the appreciation of music that lifts the mood and improves performance rather than the music itself.

Austrian musician

Wolfgang Amadeus Mozart (1756–91) could play the harpsichord aged four and compose music aged five.

Uptempo, uplifting music can improve performance, while slower, more melancholy pieces may do the opposite.

Which countries have the longest and the shortest national anthems?

MUSICAL FIRST

Nearly 40 years before Mozart penned his first opera, English poet John Gay wrote *The Beggar's Opera*, the first musical show to mix song and dialogue. With ordinary people and catchy tunes, it poked fun at the politics and social injustice of the time.

US singer Elvis Presley (1935–77) is the biggest-selling music artist of all time – no wonder 80,000 people make a living from emulating "the King of Rock and Roll".

THERE ARE ENOUGH ELVIS IMPERSONATORS TO FILL SHANGHAI STADIUM

FAST FACTS

BEETHOVEN WAS DEAF

Ludwig van Beethoven (1770–1827) was another child prodigy. But this musical marvel began to go deaf at the age of just 25, and wrote some of his best-known works, including the Ninth Symphony, without being able to hear them.

The rest is history

WONDERS OF THE ANCIENT WORLD

1. **Great Pyramid of Giza**, Egypt, built c 2500 BCE

2. **Hanging Gardens of Babylon**, Iraq, built c 600 BCE

3. **Statue of Zeus at Olympia**, Greece, carved by the sculptor Phidias c 435 BCE

4. **Temple of Artemis at Ephesus**, Turkey, destroyed by Gothic tribes in 262 CE

5. **Mausoleum at Halicarnassus**, tomb of King Mausolus, Turkey, built c 350 CE

6. **Colossus of Rhodes**, a giant statue of the Sun god Helios, built in 280 BCE

7. **Lighthouse of Alexandria**, Egypt, destroyed in 1365 CE

FIVE TYPES OF GOVERNMENT

MONARCHY — The head of state is a monarch (king or queen).

REPUBLIC — The head of state is usually an elected president.

THEOCRACY — A state governed by a religious leader or leaders.

DICTATORSHIP — A state ruled by a single person who may have seized power by force or been elected unopposed.

SINGLE-PARTY STATE — A state governed by one political party where no other parties are allowed to put up candidates for election.

A JUMBO TASK

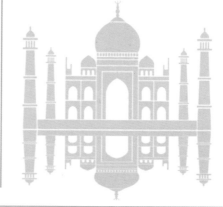

The marble and stone used to build the Taj Mahal in Agra, India, in the **17th century,** were carried there by **1,000 elephants**.

GREAT CITIES

Many places have held the title of world's biggest city – and their populations keep getting bigger!

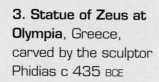

	Thebes (Egypt) Xian (China) 50,000 people	Nineveh (Iraq) 120,000 people	Babylon (Iraq) 200,000 people	Chang'an (China) 400,000 people		Rome (Italy) 450,000 people	Constantinople (Turkey) 300,000 people	Constantinople (Turkey) 400,000 people	Ctesiphon (Iraq) 500,000 people	Baghdad (Iraq) 700,000 people	Cordoba (Spain) 450,000 people
800 BCE		650 BCE	400 BCE	200 BCE	100 BCE		350 CE	500 CE	625 CE	800 CE	1000

Time to cross the Atlantic:

SHRINKING WORLD

SAILING SHIP, 1600 – 2 MONTHS

OCEAN LINER, 2014 – 7 DAYS

PASSENGER AIRPLANE, 2014 – 8 HOURS

FASTEST PASSENGER AIRPLANE (CONCORDE), 1996 – 2 HOURS, 53 MINUTES

THE FIRST **TRANSATLANTIC TELEPHONE** CALL WAS MADE FROM LONDON, UK, TO NEW YORK, USA, ON **7 MARCH 1926**.

BIG **STADIUMS**

The Circus Maximus used for chariot racing in ancient Rome, Italy, held **300,000 people**. This is twice the capacity of the largest stadium in the world today in Pyongyang, North Korea.

MIGHTY AZTECS

IN **1519**, THE AZTEC CAPITAL OF **TENOCHTITLAN** HAD **250,000** INHABITANTS – **FIVE** TIMES LARGER THAN **LONDON, UK**, AT THE TIME.

REVOLTING WORLD

History is rife with revolutions. Here are just five of the best (or worst, depending on whose side you are on):

American Revolution (1775–1783): 13 colonies throw off British rule to become the United States of America.

French Revolution (1789–1799): Monarchy is abolished, the king loses his head, and France becomes a republic.

Chinese Revolution (1911): China's last imperial dynasty, the Qing, is overthrown and China forms a republic

Russian Revolution (1917): Revolutionaries topple the tsar (emperor) and set up a communist government.

Iranian Revolution (1989): An Islamic republic is set up in Iran after the shah (king) is deposed.

ROMAN STATUES WERE MADE WITH **DETACHABLE HEADS,** SO THAT ONE HEAD COULD BE **REMOVED** AND **REPLACED** WITH ANOTHER.

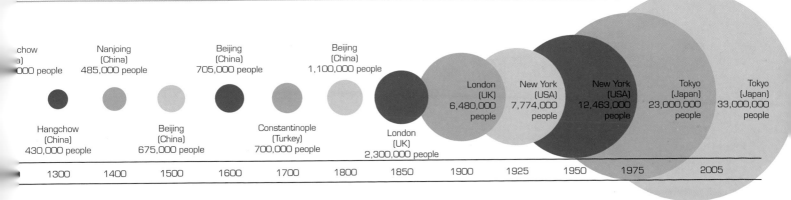

...chow (...a) ...00 people	Nanjoing (China) 485,000 people		Beijing (China) 705,000 people		Beijing (China) 1,100,000 people		London (UK) 6,480,000 people	New York (USA) 7,774,000 people	New York (USA) 12,463,000 people	Tokyo (Japan) 23,000,000 people	Tokyo (Japan) 33,000,000 people	
Hangchow (China) 430,000 people		Beijing (China) 675,000 people		Constantinople (Turkey) 700,000 people		London (UK) 2,300,000 people						
1300	1400	1500	1600	1700	1800	1850	1900	1925	1950	1975	2005	

ANSWERS

HUMAN BODY

6–7 BODILY FLUIDS
Yes. Water intoxication results in the brain swelling, with potentially fatal consequences.

8–9 THE BRAIN
No. There is no proof of this.

10–11 NERVOUS SYSTEM
90 per cent.

12–13 CIRCULATION
Yes. When you have a hot drink, nerve receptors in the tongue signal to the brain that something hot is entering the body, so it can prepare to start sweating.

14–15 DIGESTION
Yes, but only in an extreme situation of over-eating.

16–17 BONES
The feet. Each foot consists of 26 bones.

18–19 MUSCLES
Yes. Especially when you see someone else smiling, your brain's mirror neurons will stimulate a sensation that is associated with smiling, so you smile immediately.

20–21 EYES
All blue-eyed people can be traced back to one ancestor who lived 10,000 years ago near the Black Sea.

22–23 TASTE AND SMELL
Both the human tongue and an elephant's trunk are made of a muscle called a muscular hydrostat. This means that they function without help from the skeleton.

24–25 HAIR
Red hair is the least common, owned by only 1–2 per cent of the global population. This colour is mainly found in Scotland and Ireland.

26–27 ILLNESS
Exposure to bright light – photic sneezing, a condition inherited from parents.

28–29 EFFECTS OF FOOD
Vitamin D boosts bone density and prevents osteoporosis. Milk and cereals are excellent sources, but sunlight boosts levels of Vitamin D naturally as well.

30–31 GENETICS
People born after 1955 have traces of radioactive carbon in their DNA. This is left over from when the USA and USSR set off nuclear warheads during the Cold War, causing radioactivity to enter the atmosphere.

32–33 GROWTH AND AGEING
Long life.

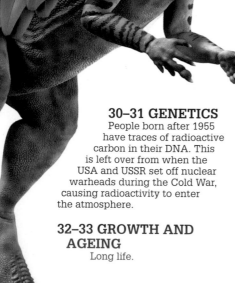

NATURE

38–39 ANIMAL EVOLUTION
On their legs.

40–41 DINOSAURS
On screen. In the film *Jurassic Park*, some of the main noises for the T-rex came from the sound designer's tiny Jack Russell terrier, Buster. The sounds were slowed down.

42–43 REPTILES
Heat is released through the crocodile's mouth.

44–45 ANIMAL BEHAVIOUR
Elephants can hear low frequency calls of other elephants that are up to 10 km (6 miles) away. The calls are too low for humans to hear, but the elephants can "hear" the sounds through their feet.

46–47 ANIMAL ADAPTATIONS
10 minutes.

48–49 DANGEROUS ANIMALS
Their ability to see very well in low light.

50–51 ANIMAL MARKINGS
Tigers and zebras.

52–53 BIRDS
Although they can't fly, ostriches can run at speeds of 60 kph (40 mph), which is as fast as a horse.

54–55 RODENTS
They never stop growing.

56–57 STINGING INSECTS
They live on every continent apart from Antarctica.

58–59 FISH
Goldfish prevent the spread of the West Nile virus. They are added to stagnant bodies of water where they eat mosquito larvae, which live in the water. This reduces mosquito populations.

60–61 INSECT FEATS
Cockroaches resist the harmful effects of radiation. They are much more likely to survive a nuclear explosion than humans, though if they were near nuclear ground zero, they would be crisped along with everything else.

62–63 SPIDERS
Up to 20 years.

64–65 FLOWERS
A number of plants are poisonous to cats, including lilies, yellow jasmine, tulip bulbs, sweet peas, and mistletoe. If you have a cat or are thinking of getting one, ensure you don't have these plants in the garden.

66–67 FRUIT AND VEGETABLES
It has an awful smell, often compared to rotting meat.

SCIENCE AND TECHNOLOGY

72–73 WATER
Morocco.

74–75 LIGHT
Iceland.

76–77 SOUND
At many European operas, whistling means "Boo!"

78–79 COLOUR
Blue. In a survey of people around the world, 40 per cent of people chose blue. The second favourite was purple, which was chosen by 14 per cent of people.

80–81 GRAVITY
A skydiver reaches 210 kph (130 mph), a tennis ball 95 kph (60 mph), and a raindrop 25 kph (15 mph).

82–83 MATHS AND PROBABILITY
Up to five times!

84–85 ELECTRICITY
American inventor Thomas Edison (1847–1931).

86–87 MATERIALS
The ancient Romans.

88–89 INVENTIONS
Penicillin was in short supply, so a global search for a more productive strain of the mould got underway. In 1943 a laboratory worker found a rotting melon in a market. It became the main source of antibiotics for the next decade.

90–91 MODERN PHYSICS
Clocks run more quickly at higher altitudes because they experience a weaker gravitational force than clocks on Earth's surface. This is known as gravitational time dilation.

92–93 THE DIGITAL AGE
Asia, with more than one billion users (44 per cent of the total).

94–95 TECHNOLOGY
Yes, it has been proven that installing CCTV cameras and reminding people that they are being watched reduces petty crimes, such as dropping litter.

96–97 ROBOTS
One in every 10 car production workers is a robot.

SPACE

102–103 BIRTH OF THE UNIVERSE
Theories about how the Universe might end – in a Big Rip (torn apart), a Big Crunch (stops expanding and collapses), or a Big Freeze (a long, slow fade-out).

104–105 EXPANDING UNIVERSE
At least 3,500 planets have been found, in addition to Earth and its neighbouring planets.

106–107 BLACK HOLES
As you get close to the hole you feel its pull. If you are going in feet first, the pull is stronger on your feet than your head. You get stretched longways, and squashed sideways, becoming increasingly long and thin – a process known as spaghettification. You are spaghettified until your body can take no more and rips apart.

108–109 GAS GIANTS
The blue comes from methane gas in their atmospheres.

110–111 ROCKY PLANETS
3.8 cm (1.5 in) per second.

112–113 SPACE BODIES
In 1930 11-year-old Venetia Burney from Oxford, England, suggested the name Pluto to her grandfather, who passed it on to the Lowell Observatory in the USA. When the name Pluto was chosen, he gave Venetia £5 as a reward.

114–115 PLANET EARTH
The high is 57.8°C (136°F) and the low is -93.2°C (-135.8°F). The average surface temperature is 15°C (59°F).

116–117 THE MOON
When Earth is directly between the Sun and the Moon, it stops sunlight reaching the Moon. The Moon is in Earth's shadow and is eclipsed. It has a reddish glow due to the scattering of sunlight as this passes through Earth's atmosphere.

118–119 THE SUN
In summer, in northerly latitudes such as northern Scandinavia, northern Canada, and northern Russia.

120–121 STARS
Scientists estimate there are 10 times more stars in the night sky than grains of sand in the world's deserts and beaches.

122–123 ASTRONOMY
Either because the star creates more light, is closer to Earth, or a combination of both.

124–125 SPACE TRAVEL
Due to the weightlessness in Space, dust does not settle down. As it just floats around, astronauts sneeze a lot.

EARTH

130–131 PLATE TECTONICS
The average thickness of a tectonic plate is 80 km (50 miles).

132–133 OCEANS
Russia, the USA, Canada, and Australia.

134–135 RIVERS
In 1988 school students in Montana, USA, successfully campaigned to have their local North Fork Roe River recognized as the world's shortest. It is just 18 m (59 ft) long.

136–137 MOUNTAINS
A peak above 610 m (2,000 ft) is a mountain, while anything smaller is a hill.

138–139 DESERTS
The hottest desert is the Sahara, while the coldest is Antarctica.

140–141 VOLCANOES
Volcano Toba exploded 73,000 years ago in what is now Indonesia.

142–143 EARTHQUAKES
Yes – underwater.

144–145 THE SEASONS
Earth takes time to warm up or cool down. Therefore, the seasons lag behind. The amount of lag is affected by factors such as distance from the poles, amounts of water surrounding the area, and the weather experienced during the year.

146–147 WEATHER PREDICTION
When seagulls stop flying, avoid water, and huddle on the ground together, it is usually a sign of wet weather.

148–149 THUNDERSTORMS
The hairs on your body stand up.

150–151 SNOW
No. Below -30°C (-22°F) there is not usually enough moisture in the cold air for snow, but it is possible. Snow has fallen at -41°C (-41.8°F).

152–153 POPULATION
China.

HISTORY AND CULTURE

158–159 PREHISTORIC PEOPLE
Flutes made of bones and tusks have been discovered, showing that Neanderthals played music.

160–161 ANCIENT EGYPT
A total of 2,300,000 stone blocks make up the Great Pyramid.

162–163 ANCIENT GREECE
Some paint was made of lead, and this is hazardous. It can cause damage to the nervous system, kidney failure, and stunted growth.

164–165 ANCIENT ROME
Purple was considered the colour of status and authority, so only the Emperor could wear it. The purple dye came from the shell of a sea snail called a murex.

166–167 THE VIKINGS
Skiing. The Vikings enjoyed skiing and worshipped a god of skiing named Ullr.

168–169 THE MIDDLE AGES
Water. This mostly came from wells, so would have been relatively clean. Peasants also drank beer, which was much weaker than it is today. Wine was the drink of choice in noble households.

170–171 DISEASES
Some villages killed off all their cats because they were supposedly associated with witchcraft. Without cats to keep rat numbers down, the population grew and the Plague spread even more quickly.

172–173 EXPLORATION
Amnesty (an official pardon) was granted to criminals who went on the dangerous journey. At least four men are known to have taken advantage of the offer.

174–175 THE FRENCH REVOLUTION
About 300.

176–177 LEADERS
Nelson Mandela. In 2013 the prehistoric woodpecker *Australopicus nelsonmandelai* was named after him.

178–179 WORLD WAR
About six weeks, with junior officers and stretcher-carriers most vulnerable.

180–181 OLYMPIC SPORT
They competed naked.

182–183 FOOD
The test-tube burger is the world's most expensive, at £250,000 ($385,000). It was made in a Netherlands laboratory from 20,000 strips of synthetic "cultured beef" taken from cow stem cells.

184–185 MUSIC
The shortest is the text of the Japanese anthem, *Kimigayo*, with only 32 characters. The longest is the Greek anthem, "*Hymn to Liberty*", which has 158 verses.

INDEX

ACKNOWLEDGEMENTS

DK would like to thank: John Searcy for Americanization; Carron Brown for the index and proofreading; Fran Baines for editorial assistance; Simon Mumford for maps; Stefan Podhorodecki for photographing the Marie Antoinette cake and Rosalind Miller for making the cake www.rosalindmillercakes.com.

The publisher would like to thank the following for their kind permission to reproduce their photographs:

(Key: a-above; b-below/bottom; c-centre; f-far; l-left; r-right; t-top)

1 Dreamstime.com: John Kasawa (b). 2 Getty Images: Arctic-Images / Stone (br). Science Photo Library: CDC / Science Source (tr). 3 Alamy Images: Conspectus (cl). Corbis: Frans Lanting (cb). Dreamstime.com: Alena Stalmashonak (cra). NASA: ESA (tc). 4–5 Science Photo Library: CDC / Science Source. 6 Dreamstime.com: Subhash Pathrakkada Balan (br). 8 Science Photo Library: Dr. Scott T. Grafton, Visuals Unlimited (cl). 10–11 Getty Images: Jonathan Kitchen / Photodisc (c). 10 Corbis: Visuals Unlimited (tc). 11 iStockphoto.com: Firstsignal (tc). 12–13 Science Photo Library: Dr. Arthur Tucker (t). 12 Alamy Images: Images&Stories (crb). 14 Science Photo Library: Springer Medizin (br). 16-17 Dorling Kindersley: Geoff Brightling / ESPL - modelmaker (t). Dreamstime.com: Georgii Dolgykh (cb). 16 Science Photo Library: (br). 17 Alamy Images: DR Studio (cr). 18–19 Alamy Images: SuperStock / Purestock (c). 18 Getty Images: BSIP / Universal Images Group (clb). 20 Science Photo Library: Pasieka (bl). 20–21 Dreamstime.com: Gabriel Blaj (c). 22–23 Alamy Images: Estiot / BSIP (c). 22 Science Photo Library: Prof. P. Motta / Dept. Of Anatomy / University "La Sapienza", Rome (clb). 23 Dreamstime.com: Dimakp (clb). 24 Science Photo Library: Eye Of Science (clb). 24–25 Dreamstime.com: Stefan Hermans (bc). 25 Dreamstime.com: Miramisska (tl). 26 Dreamstime.com: Alexander Raths (cb). 28 Dreamstime.com: Antonio De Azevedo Negrão (cl). 30 Dreamstime.com: Paul Fleet (clb). 31 Corbis: John Lund / Blend Images (ca/cow); Solvin Zankl / Visuals Unlimited (ca); Allan Stone. Dreamstime.com: Ajn (cla). 32–33 Dreamstime.com: Eldadcarin (c). 32 Corbis: Pascal Parrot / Sygma (clb). 36–37 Getty Images: Arctic-Images / Stone. 38 Dreamstime.com: Filip Fuxa (tc). 40 Dreamstime.com: Robert Wisdom (bl). 40–41 Dorling Kindersley: Andrew Kerr (c).

41 Corbis: Louie Psihoyos (br). 42–43 Dreamstime.com: John Kasawa (b). 42 Corbis: Bence Mate / Nature Picture Library (cl). 44–45 Dreamstime.com: Bolotov (Yellow post-it). 44 Getty Images: Barcroft Media (bl). Dreamstime.com: Sharon Day. 46–47 Dreamstime.com: Kanokphoto (b). 46 Getty images: GK Hart/Vicky Hart /Stone 47 Dreamstime.com: Benham001 (tc). 48–49 SeaPics.com: James D. Watt. 48 Corbis: Flip Nicklin / Minden Pictures (r). 50–51 Getty Images: Joel Sartore / National Geographic. 51 Corbis: Alex Wild / Visuals Unlimited (tr). 52–53 Alamy Images: Steve Bloom. 52 Dreamstime.com: Wayne Mckown (clb). 54–55 Dreamstime.com: Cynoclub (bc). 54 SuperStock: Juniors (cl). 55 Dreamstime.com: Christian Draghici (c). 56–57 Dreamstime.com: Katrina Brown (c). 56 Corbis: Erik De Castro / Reuters (bl). Dreamstime.com: Alfio Scisetti (br). 58–59 Dreamstime.com: Elena Torre (bc); Monika Wisniewska (c). 58 Dreamstime.com: Sekarb (bl). 60 Manchester X-ray Imaging Facility: Tristan Lowe (bl). 61 Dreamstime.com: Tofuxs (bl). SuperStock: imagebroker.ne (c). 62 Getty Images: Stephen Dalton / Minden Pictures (cb); Steven Taylor / The Image Bank (clb). SuperStock: imagebroker.net (bl). 62–63 Alamy Images: Juniors Bildarchiv / F259 (c). Getty Images: Space Images / Blend Images (b). 63 Getty Images: Aaron Ansarov / Aurora (crb). Science Photo Library: Gerry Pearce (ca). 65 Dreamstime.com: Alfio Scisetti (c). Getty Images: Tom Cockrem / Photolibrary (tr). 66 Corbis: 735 / Tom Merton / Ocean (bl). 67 Getty Images: Creative Crop / Digital Vision (c). Pearson Asset Library: Cheuk-king Lo (bl). 70 Alamy Images: Conspectus. 72 Getty Images: Carin Krasner / Photodisc (tc). Robert Harding Picture Library: Paul Springett / Still Pictures (br). 73 Dreamstime.com: Emicristea. 74–75 Dreamstime.com: Yongnian Gui. 75 Dorling Kindersley: Rough Guides (tr). 76 Alamy Images: Ricardo Funari / BrazilPhotos (tl). 77 Alamy Images: Comstock Production Department / Comstock Images (bc). Corbis: Mike Kemp / Rubberball (t). 78 Dreamstime.com: Andyhighlander (clb). 80 Alamy Images: speedpix (tc). 81 Alamy Images: Carlos Hernandez / Westend61 GmbH. Dreamstime.com: Gradts (c). 82 Dreamstime.com: Selectphoto (bl). 83 123RF.com: Jordan Tan (cb). 84–85 Dreamstime.com: Ahmad Zaihan Amran (c); Thommeo (c/computer screen). 84 Dreamstime.com: Ulina Tauer (clb). 85 Corbis: National Geographic Society (crb). 86 Alamy Images:

Wayne Simpson / All Canada Photos (br). 90 Corbis: Bettmann (clb). 92–93 123RF.com: Anton Balazh (c). 92 Getty Images: artpartner-images / The Image Bank (clb). 94 Getty Images: Toussaint Kluiters / AFP (bl). 95 Getty Images: Daniel Berehulak (Screens). 96 Corbis: Ina Fassbender / X00970 / Reuters (bl); Photo Japan / Robert Harding World Imagery (r). Dreamstime.com: Anankkml (t). Getty Images: Peter Macdiarmid (bc). 96–97 Dreamstime.com: Esviesa (b). 97 123RF.com: (bc); Viktoriya Sukhanova (bl). Dreamstime.com: Ruslan Gilmanshin (cb). Getty Images: Spencer Platt (br). 100 NASA: ESA. 102 Getty Images: Panoramic Images (bc). 102–103 ESA / Hubble: NASA/S. Beckwith (STScI)/HUDF Team/http://creative commons.org/licenses/by/3.0 (Background). Science Photo Library: Mark Garlick. 104 NASA: M.J. Jee / Johns Hopkins University (clb). 106 Dreamstime.com: Leonello Calvetti (tr); Chernetskiy (bc). NASA: (bl). 107 Dreamstime.com: Isselee (bc); Andres Rodriguez (tl). 108 Dorling Kindersley: NASA / JPL (bl). 109 Pascal Henry, www.lesud.com. 110-111 Corbis: NASA / JPL-Caltech. 110 NASA: JPL (clb). 112 Pascal Henry, www.lesud.com: (bl). 113 Corbis: Denis Scott (cb). Dreamstime.com: Dave Bredeson (c); Odua (clb). ESO: L. Calçada and Nick Risinger (skysurvey.org)/http://creative commons.org/licenses/by/3.0 (bc). NASA: (bl). 114 Corbis: Esa / epa (bl). Dreamstime.com: Rtguest. 116 Dreamstime.com: Fang Jia (bc). NASA: Goddard / Arizona State University (cl). Science Photo Library: Geoeye (clb). 118 Fotolia: dundanim (bl). Science Photo Library: Greg Piepol (clb). 119 Dreamstime.com: Rastan (r). 120 ESA / Hubble: NASA/http:// creativecommons.org/licenses/by/3.0 (bl). 123 ESA / Hubble: NASA/http:// creativecommons.org/licenses/by/3.0 (cr). Science Photo Library: David Nunuk (br). 124 Corbis: NASA / Roger Ressmeyer (clb). 125 Dorling Kindersley: NASA (b). 128 Corbis: Frans Lanting. 130 Alamy Images: Chris Howes / Wild Places Photography (clb). Fotolia: Shchipkova Elena (bc). 131 PunchStock: Photodisc / Paul Souders (bl). 132 Corbis: Bettmann (bl). 134 Corbis: 145 / Sylvain Cordier / Ocean (cl). 136–137 Dreamstime.com: Andreykuzmin (b). 136 Alamy Images: Stelios Michael (bl). Dreamstime.com: Anke Van Wyk (cl); Sergii Gnatiuk (cl/trophy). 137 Dreamstime.com: Axel2001 (c). NASA: MOLA Science Team / O. de Goursac, Adrian Lark (tl). 138 Corbis: Colin Monteath / Hedgehog House /

Minden Pictures (clb). 140 Dorling Kindersley: Rough Guides (bl). Dreamstime.com: Toadberry (br). 140–141 Corbis: Richard Roscoe / Stocktrek Images. 142 Corbis: Alison Wright. 145 Corbis: ibrahim ibrahim / Demotix (cr). 146–147 Corbis: Image Source. 147 Getty Images: Science & Society Picture Library (tc). 148 Getty Images: Michael Siward / Moment. Science Photo Library: Dr. John Brackenbury (clb). 149 Getty Images: Michael Siward / Moment. 150 Alamy Images: Whit Richardson (clb). Corbis: 68 / Cavan Images / Ocean (br). Dreamstime.com: James Steidl (cb). 151 Corbis: 68 / Cavan Images / Ocean (bc). Dreamstime.com: Rita Jayaraman (c). 152 Corbis: Bertrand Rieger / Hemis (br). 156 Alamy Images: Jon Arnold Images Ltd. 158 Science Photo Library: James King-Holmes (clb). 160 Getty Images: AFP (bl). 162 akg-images: John Hios (r). Corbis: Ali Kabas (bl). 163 akg-images: John Hios (l). 164 Corbis: Fred de Noyelle / Godong. 166–167 Tom Banwell Designs 2008. 167 Getty Images: AFP (bc). 169 Getty Images: Turkish School / The Bridgeman Art Library (cr). 170 Alamy Images: Pictorial Press Ltd (bl). 172–173 Dorling Kindersley: Ian Cummings / Rough Guides (t); Greg Ward and James McConnachie / Rough Guides (b). 172 Dreamstime.com: Seagames50 (clb). 173 The Bridgeman Art Library: Science Museum, London, UK (c). 174–175 Dorling Kindersley: Marie Antoinette and Rosalind Miller – cake maker / Stefan Podhorodecki (c). 175 Corbis: The Gallery Collection (br). 176 Alamy Images: Lebrecht Music and Arts Photo Library (br). Getty Images: De Agostini / A. Dagli Orti (clb). 177 Getty Images: Media24 / Gallo Images / Hulton Archive (bc); Central Press / Hulton Archive (br). SuperStock: Library of Congress / Science Faction (bc/Lincoln); Universal Images Group (bl). 178 Corbis: Reuters Photographer / Reuters (clb). 178–179 bnps.co.uk: (bc). Corbis: Warren Faidley (t); Creativ Studio Heinemann / Westend61 (b). 180 Getty Images: Milos Bicanski (clb). 182 Alamy Images: World History Archive / Image Asset Management Ltd. (bl). 182–183 Dreamstime.com: Nevodka (bc). 183 Dreamstime.com: Photographerlondon (c); Winai Tepsuttinun (c/America flag toothpick). 184 Getty Images: Carlos Alvarez / E+ (c). 184–185 Corbis: The Gallery Collection. 185 Alamy Images: Peter Barritt (bl)

All other images © Dorling Kindersley

For further information see: www.dkimages.com